# THE TRIANGLE OF THE SOUL

### Find More Fulfillment in Life

### LaMar Prince

PrinceWriter Publishing Company

Princewriter.com

PrinceWriter Publishing Company

Charlotte, N.C. 28273

www.princewriter.com

Copyright ©2012 by LaMar Prince

All rights reserved, including the right to reproduce this book or portions thereof in any form whatsoever. For information contact www.princewriter.com or www.triangleofthesoul.com.

Library of Congress Cataloging-in-Publication Data available

ISBN 978-0-9884943-0-5

Visit LaMar at www.triangleofthesoul.com

This book is dedicated to my Mom….

I wish you were here to share this

experience with me.

*To my sons, Robert and Caleb,*

*Thank you for your support and encouragement. Let this book be a testimony that you can make your dreams a reality as long as you put God first, stay diligent, and believe in yourself. I love you guys more than you will ever know.*

- INTRODUCTION TO THE TRIANGLE OF THE SOUL ............7
- INTELLECTUAL SELF..................................................14
- EMOTIONAL SELF .....................................................22
- SPIRITUAL SELF........................................................30
- QUIET TIME...............................................................35
- DEALING WITH DEPRESSION....................................50
- LED BY THE SPIRIT...................................................66
- UNCOVERING HIDDEN PAINS ...................................76
- HEALING FROM HIDDEN PAINS ................................86
- HEALER OF HIDDEN PAINS.......................................96
- SPIRITUAL SELF....MORE .......................................102
- POWER TO IMPACT THE WORLD .............................114
- POWER OF FAITH ...................................................131
- POWER OF FAITH....MORE .....................................140
- GUARD YOUR SOUL.................................................150
- RECEIVING YOUR SOUL'S DESIRES........................159
- WHEN WE DIE ........................................................172

# Introduction to the
# Triangle of the Soul

# Introduction to The Triangle of the Soul

Regardless of our age, cultural background, experiences, religious or personal beliefs, at some point during life's journey, we all ask ourselves, "What is my purpose in life?" For some, this question is fueled by an unexplainable feeling of something within us that is not being fulfilled or that is out of balance. At times, we wonder if we are truly living and experiencing our lives to its fullest. Often, the seemingly best solution to this problem is to focus on acquiring the tangible things our world tells us are important. In response, we fashion our lives in the pursuit of things, and on some levels we experience success. Yet that feeling does not subside.

Consider for a moment that the keys to finding more fulfillment in life can not found in tangible things. What if the keys to finding more fulfillment in life were all around you, but you just didn't see them? What if these keys have been jingling and presenting themselves to you every day, begging you to pick them up and use them. The precious keys to finding more fulfillment exist, and they lie waiting for you within your soul.

# Introduction to The Triangle of the Soul

Your soul is the treasure chest of everything that makes you - you. It is your divinity. It is where you generate the power of thoughts, the energy of feelings, and receive spiritual urgings from the Creator. Again, your soul is divine! In this book, we will attempt to understand how the awesome and all-encompassing existence of your soul impacts every aspect of your life. And second, we will attempt to discover the keys within it to enable you find more fulfillment in your life.

The first step towards understanding and gaining a better connection to your soul is to embrace the idea that your soul is made of three parts. The three parts of your soul are the spiritual *self,* emotional *self,* and intellectual *self.* Throughout this book, we will often identify each of these parts of our soul using the word *self* because each of these parts is individually recognizable.

Although each part is individually recognizable, they are inseparable and rely on one another to exist. Picture them as a triangle. In order for a triangle to exist each of the three sides must be connected to the other two. Each side of your soul depends on the others to function. In this sense, your soul is a trinity. Perhaps

# Introduction to The Triangle of the Soul

the most common example of a trinity exists in the Christian faith. The three divine identities of power in Christianity are God, Jesus, and the Holy Spirit. Each identity of this triangle possesses the essence of the other two, all in one and inseparable. However, each identity of this trinity has somewhat different and identifiable roles.

Regardless of the roles we play or the identity we take on in the external world, we cannot quiet the divine internal voice of our soul. However, too often we find ourselves bombarded with media outlets, peer pressures, negative self-talk, and other concealed messages that work to convince us to go against the true voice of our souls. As a result, some of us live a lifetime struggling to realize our divinity and utmost fulfillment in life.

We can all recall stories of celebrities, public figures, the extraordinarily rich, or even acquaintances of people who are successful but live unfulfilled lives. When we hear stories of their self-destruction, we are often shocked with amazement. But, why? Why are we often personally impacted when the personal

## Introduction to The Triangle of the Soul

shortcomings of people we assumed had near perfect lives become public?

Another question to ask is why do they have such troubled lives? They have access to the things most of us are taught to value and admire; they are the envy of their worlds, the best of us. So why are they so unfulfilled in life?

Deeper questions to ask are why does it seem the things that should make us feel happy and complete often fall short or only last temporarily? Why do so many of us live in a perpetual struggle to maintain happiness (as if it doesn't want to be a part of our lives), an existence where fulfillment in life seems impossible.

*An unhappy, unfulfilled life is evidence of a soul that is out of balance.* In this world, fulfillment in life is only possible when there are balance and true awareness of the state of our intellectual, emotional, and spiritual self. Working toward obtaining and maintaining this state within the soul is the essence of happiness. Perhaps, one of our greatest sins is that we willingly choose to establish imbalance within *the triangle of the soul.*

# Introduction to The Triangle of the Soul

In this book, we will not contemplate the existence of God, neither will we try to postulate God in the context of any specific religious belief; we will simply assume that God exists. Very often we will refer to God as the Creator. Here's why. As humans, we cannot truly create anything; we can only change its form. For example, we can combine preexisting elements to form plastics and cement and fashion them with wood to build a house; but we cannot create a house from nothing. Only a *true creator* has the ability to make something from absolutely nothing; therefore, the title of the Creator denotes ultimate power, wisdom, and required adoration - God.

From the moment of your birth to your last breaths, you will experience and impact the world through the triangle of your soul. Although the keys to finding fulfillment in life are generally the same for each of us, you have additional keys that are uniquely designed for you. These are your keys to finding *more* fulfillment in life.

Throughout our reading experience your soul will reveal keys to finding more fulfillment in your life, so keep a notepad nearby to

## Introduction to The Triangle of the Soul

write down whatever comes to you. It may be a good idea to keep a notepad designated only for this book. It will also come in handy when you arrive at chapters that will entail note taking and interaction. Also be prepared to frequently stop throughout each chapter for designated moments of reflection and *quiet time.*

Your choice to read this book at this moment in time is not by chance or accident. This is your time! Your time to find more fulfillment in life. Thank you and welcome to a life-changing reading experience.

## Intellectual Self

## Intellectual Self

Let's begin to explore deeper into the concept that our soul is not one identity but is made up of three parts. As you recall, we have identified the three separate identities of the soul; our intellectual self, emotional self, and spiritual self. We've been introduced to the idea of referring to each of these parts using the addition of the word "self" because they are, in fact, each an individual essence of who we are. Furthermore, we now know that because each of these parts depends on and supports the others, we have come to visualize them as forming a triangle. We've also introduced the idea that our souls are divine. As a result, *the triangle of the soul* is our identity in this life and is connected to a higher power.

Largely our intellectual self is recognizable and can commonly be measured and developed. It receives constant information from all of our physical senses with audio and visual providing the greatest influence. Within our intellectual self, we receive, retain and process every moment of our lives, and we use this information to expand our knowledge.

However, our intellectual self expands far beyond its data processing abilities; it also serves as the gatekeeper to practically

## Intellectual Self

all external physical stimulations received into the soul. In other words, most of what our soul knows is primarily received through our intellectual self. Our intellectual self maintains and regulates every physical function within our bodies and provides us with the principal means to interact with the world. We depend on our intellect for our very survival. Given the intellect's vital role in maintaining our survival and functionality we often over utilize it within *the triangle of the soul*.

Our intellectual self's primary purpose within the soul is to keep us connected to the physical world. In other words, it serves to keep us "worldly". Its inherent purpose is to drive us towards establishing and maintaining our existence within the psychical world. Furthermore, since our intellect primarily uses logic to process all information, it measures everything, whether tangible or intangible on measurable objects. In other words, our intellectual self measures intangible concepts such as success, happiness and even fulfillment in life on the attainment of physical possessions and accomplishments.

## Intellectual Self

*A key to finding more fulfillment in life is to stop thinking so much.* This is not a call to embrace ignorance or a putdown on logical and critical thinking, nor does this mean we should neglect our intelligence. It is a call to better understand how our intellectual self impacts our level of fulfillment and happiness in life. When we have a clearer understanding of how our intellectual self functions within the soul, the keys to finding more fulfillment in life will become more evident.

Here is an example of our intellectual self in action. Our intellect gathers information from the physical world and formulates the thought that success equals happiness. As a result, our intellect develops a definition for the word "success" based on our past experiences and our current situation. Since each of our experiences is different, our definition of an abstract concept like success will vary. Next, our intellectual self measures our personal level of success based on tangible objects that support our definitions; such as, the cars we drive, the homes we live in, the jobs we perform, level of education, and status of our relationships or children...the list is immeasurable.

## Intellectual Self

Here is another example. We all have an intellectually established definition of human beauty, and we use it to measure and compare our level of beauty or attractiveness. We use this definition to choose our mates, sometimes friends and for some to determine our self-worth. Have you ever felt nervousness while talking with someone you felt was attractive? Intellectually you measured them as more beautiful than you and thus better than you.

Our intellectual self performs countless comparisons and measurements every moment of our lives; all in an attempt to continually define our worth and status. If left unchecked, our intellectual self can quickly distort the balance within *the triangle of the soul*; our intellect's primary function is to keep us connected to the external world. As a result, we can easily find ourselves dedicating our lives toward pursuing goals and possessions that will never lead us to true happiness or fulfillment in life. Here's why. Since our world is ever changing, our definition of self-worth and the requirements to maintain a status that will provide fulfillment in life are also constantly changing. As a result, we can

## Intellectual Self

become locked into a never-ending struggle; searching for a state of being that is perpetually temporary – leaving us constantly unfulfilled.

Fortunately, there is a simple test we can take to help us determine if we are thinking too much, or in other words, if our intellectual self is out of balance within our triangle. Ask yourself the following question, "What are the most common things I pray for, think about obtaining, meditate on, or are my goals in life?" List at least five items that come to you on your notepad. Review your list. How many items on your list represent psychical things you want to *receive* versus intangible things you want to be able to *give*? If your list is dominated by physical things you want to receive, versus things you want to be able to give, then perhaps your intellectual self is out of balance within your soul. In addition, observe the balance between your focus on physical things compared to your spiritual and emotional desires.

Do not be dismayed if your list is more "worldly" than you'd like; this is one of those moments of revelation we read about earlier. Perhaps at this moment your spiritual self is revealing

## INTELLECTUAL SELF

pursuits in your life that may seem rewarding or like the right things to do, but are in fact keeping you from your true keys to finding more fulfillment in life.

Although our intellect's primary purpose is to keep us connected to the external world, it is not inherently evil; intelligence is a gift from God. Every component of the soul is designed by The Creator to enable us to experience our divinity. Without the functionality of our intellect, we would not be able to physically hear, read, understand, nor remember spiritual teachings.

*Most of our prayers derive from our intellect's connection to the physical world. Therefore, our intellectual self's importance spans beyond connecting us to this world; it also contributes to our connection to God. Needless to say, we need our intelligence, but we must remain diligently aware of how our thoughts affect our ability to find more fulfillment within the triangle of the soul.*

We must remain critically aware of the information we allow our intellectual self to be exposed to or focused on. You cannot stop yourself from learning. Intellectually you are still that bright-eyed baby, constantly gathering and processing information from the world. As a result, your level and type of learning (thinking) is constantly being formed by the information that is exposed to you. For a moment, ask your spiritual self to reveal any information you are voluntarily exposing yourself to that is detracting from your ability to experience more fulfillment in life. Write down whatever comes to you. Now, take action to remove or at least minimize that source of information from your life.

# Emotional Self

One of the most important functions of our emotional self is to enhance the connection between the intellectual and spiritual selves. As a result, it is often caught between the tangible and intangible worlds; in response, our emotional self is constantly driving us towards actions that are intended to provide us with the greatest level of comfort. In this book, "comfort" is not subjected to determining whether actions are good or bad, but simply if an action makes us *feel* good. Later, we will learn how our emotional self's need to provide our soul with a certain level of on-going comfort can sometimes result in destructive outcomes known as *hidden pains*.

Our emotional self is not capable nor was it designed to be our lead decision-maker. Again, this is because our emotions will always drive us to take actions that will provide us with the greatest level of comfort, with little regard for the process or consequences. Procrastination is a great example. For a moment, recall a situation upon which you procrastinated. Moments before you decided to delay addressing that situation; your intellectual self gave you a logical list of the tasks you needed to complete. Almost immediately, your emotional self sensed the discomfort you might experience and convinced you to delay taking on that project. You were fully aware that action needed to be taken and that delaying its pursuit would most likely cause more stress in the future – but your emotions did not care! Your emotional self's only concern was to present you with a solution that would lead you towards comfort.

Is there a difficult task in your life you are trying to accomplish but for some reason you can't seem to stay motivated to complete? Perhaps your emotional self is driving you to stay comfortable. Remember your emotions were not designed to be your lead decision maker. An unbalanced position of authority led by your emotional self will certainly hinder your ability to find more fulfillment in life.

Most of the impulsive decisions we make are driven by our emotional self's need to provide the soul with some level of comfort. Impulsive actions such as taking revenge, lashing out in anger, cheating, lying; the list goes on, are most often the results of allowing our emotional self to be our primary decision-maker.

Have you ever felt torn when you were faced with making a difficult decision? Perhaps you've said, "My head is saying one thing, while my heart is telling me another." That statement was truer than you might have realized! During those confusing situations, your intellectual self was giving you the best logical option, while your emotions were trying to convince you to take whatever actions that would make you feel the most comfortable. *Indecisiveness is an indication that the triangle of the soul is out of balance.* We experience indecisiveness when we fail to listen to or trust the leadership of the Creator, who speaks to us through urging from our spiritual self.

One of the most effective ways to enhance the voice of our spiritual self is through *quiet time*. Quiet time allows our emotional self to calm down and regain its place of balance with *the triangle of the soul*. When properly balanced, our emotions play an invaluable role in our decision-making process because it empowers us to understand the intangible impact of our choices. In its proper place, our emotions will cause our intellect to calculate a possible solution more broadly; we may even consider illogical the greater good. A great example is self-sacrifice.

Through its connection to our intellectual self, our emotions gain access to the external world. This connection is our ability to express feelings. Emotions also enhance our connection to the external world by providing our intellect with the ability to interrupt illogical or hidden expressions, such as, when someone is attracted to you or is lying. This connection can be also displayed through our ability to be creative.

Our emotional self is uniquely divine because it is much more likely to accept influences from the spiritual part of our soul. Remember, our intellectual self is designed to interpret the world from a physical, logical perspective. As a result, our intellect is less likely to accept the intangible. This is why the illogical concept of faith is often opposed by the intellect. Most often we need our emotions to convince our intellectual self to accept ideas that cannot be proven. On its own, our intellectual self cannot accept the fact of an Almighty God. We experience God within our soul, first through our spiritual self; this influences our emotions, which persuades our intellect. This is why God cannot be logically explained, but is deeply felt. We will explore more deeply into this process later in the chapter entitled, *The Power of Faith*.

Have you ever experienced feelings that cannot be reasonably explained? Feelings, which defy logic, some of which may even drive you to perform deeds that go beyond your normal limits? They may be an overwhelming need to be generous, forgiving, thoughtful, or to perform other acts of charity. Perhaps you've experienced unexplained feelings of joy, hope or peace in the midst of a bad situation. Perhaps you've had the experience of sensing unforeseen danger or that something dreadful is happening to a loved one. These unexplained feelings manifest themselves through our emotional self's connection to our spirit. This is a hint of the divine nature of our soul.

It is extremely important to understand that our emotions are indiscriminate. This explains why we can experience and express genuine emotional reactions to events we know are not real. For instance, have you ever cheered when the bad-guy finally got what they deserved at the climax of a movie or fought to pull back your tears during a sad scene? During those moments, our intellect clearly understands that the events on the screen are not real, but our emotional self could not keep itself from experiencing their influence.

The goal of entertainment, advertisement, sales techniques, speeches and most other media outreach programs are to cause you to experience manufactured emotional responses that will drive you to act in their favor. They understand unchecked emotions can drive you towards acting irresponsible actions. Again, your emotions were not designed to be your lead decision maker.

More concerning, is the fact that we are seldom aware of the external forces that influence our emotions. Sadly, many of us continually repeat destructive behaviors because we are unaware of the driving forces that cause us to feel a certain way about a situation. Poor eating habits and impulsive spending are two common examples. What is your soul revealing to you at this moment? What actions in your life are being driven by manufactured or unchecked emotional feelings? Write them down.

## Emotional Self

Whatever came to you are some of the situations that are keeping you from finding more fulfillment in life. Later in the chapters titled *Quiet Time* and *Uncovering Hidden Pains,* we will learn how to perform a more extensive inventory of our emotional self.

Your emotions are both divine and carnal. They can amplify the urging of your spirit as well as push your intellect to greater heights of achievements. Your emotions express the condition of the soul. Although you have complete control over your emotions, your feelings are always true and undeniable. What are you feeling right now? Even more, what emotional expressions seem to dominate in your life? Do you see areas that are in need of change? Are they impeding your ability to experience more fulfillment in life? Keep reading!

## SPIRITUAL SELF

## Spiritual Self

The least obvious and thus most perplexing component of the soul is our spiritual self. Throughout time, the concept or even existence of a spiritual self has been debated, studied, mystically and logically deduced. Within *the triangle of the soul,* your spiritual self is the essence of God existing within you; it is God's eternal breath of life. "And God breathed the breath of life into man, and man became a living soul," Genesis 2:7 KNV. The breath of God is the foundation of your divinity; it places you above all other living creatures, even angels.

Another way to look at your spiritual self is to think of it as the fingerprints left on your soul by the potter's hands while your soul was being shaped. As a result, all humans bear the mark of God on their souls. This mark gives us the ability to connect with The Creator. Through the connection of our spiritual self, God hears our voice and more importantly, we are able to hear the Creator's voice.

In this book, we will not contemplate who has the right to proclaim fellowship with God. Instead, we will focus on the fact that every human is created in the image of God by virtue of the fact we all have a spirit. God is a spirit; to be created in God's image is to have a spirit. The existence of a spiritual self gives us a soul. Other creatures may possess intelligence and display emotions, but no other creature has the image of the Creator living within them, only humans have *the triangle of the soul*.

It is impossible for your spiritual self to be directly influenced by the external world because the external world is tangible and your spirit is not. Evil thoughts and feelings are conceived and developed by your thoughts and emotions; thereby evil enters and resides within the soul. Your spiritual self cannot be corrupted by evil (it is purely divine) but your soul can. We will learn later in the chapter titled, *When We Die*, that your soul as a whole can be punished with damnation.

If a part of our soul is incorruptible, then how is it we are capable of committing evil acts? We have the godly ability to choose. On the surface, that sounds like an obvious statement, but think about it; there is no other power in the Universe, not even the Creator can (or will) make you choose to do good or evil. You can be tempted beyond imagination, your body can be tortured to levels of pain unknown throughout time, and you still have ability whether to do good or evil! Even if you believe that a soul can be possessed by another spirit, that spirit can only enter a soul that allows it in. *A key to finding fulfillment in life is truly embracing the fact that you have a choice.* God Almighty gave you the ultimate power over the triangle of your soul – you are solely responsible for all of your thoughts, emotions, and the awareness of your spirit. Regardless of how you view yourself or your place in this world, there is absolutely no power known or unknown that can separate you from your divine connection to God – except you.

Your ultimate guide to experiencing more fulfillment in life is your spiritual self's never-ending connection to God. Regardless of the condition of your soul the Creator is always present and reaching out to guide and empower you through your spiritual self. Sadly, this most critically important component of our soul is often the most neglected. My sincerest desire is as you enhance your understanding of *the triangle of the soul*, you will begin to recognize and capitalize on the awesome power of your spiritual self.

## Spiritual Self

See your soul as a triangle with each part or side connected and dependent on the other. Remember, your intellectual self's primary role is to connect you to the external (tangible) world; your spiritual self connects you to the eternal (intangible) world, and on this level, your emotions serve as a link between the two.

Perhaps while reading these past three chapters, you have begun to see areas in your life that are hindering your ability to find more fulfillment in life. If this is true, please do not allow those life-changing revelations to slip away. At the end of each chapter or whenever you feel the need have a few moments of quiet time, review your notes and write down whatever additional revelations revealed to you. In our next chapter, entitled *Quiet Time*, we will begin to uncover methods that will aid us in our mission to become more aware of the triangle of the soul, the Creator and how to find more fulfillment in life.

## Quiet Time

## Quiet Time

It seems too often throughout our "always on" lifestyles, we find ourselves desperately trying to capture that elusive feeling of fulfillment or even balance in life. These treasures are seldom found because we have been taught to neglect our spiritual self. Many of us accept the idea that we have a spirit, however; the thought of it truly being an active participant in our daily lives eludes us.

The primary function of our spiritual self is to enable us to connect with God. *When we enhance our connection to the Creator, balance within the soul and fulfillment in life can be the only result.* Our spiritual self is an important component of *the triangle of the soul* and should have an equal presence within our lives.

However, for most of us, our souls have grown into scalene triangles (each side is different in length). In other words, one side of the triangle of the soul has become more dominant than the other two; a soul that is out of balance. An unbalanced emotional presence within the soul can be witnessed when we lash out with exaggerated responses to mundane inconveniences. Long-lasting feelings of depression, anger, frustration, and a host of ill-conceived actions such as revenge or the lack of mercy for others are a few symptoms of a soul that is disproportionally controlled by our emotions.

The role of our intellectual self is to connect us to the external world; however, when this connection is out of balance, we begin to develop a type of tunnel vision and are self-absorbed. This imbalance resides in our rationality of selfishness. Selfishness is not always the spoiled brat lexicon we have attributed it. Merriam-Webster defines the word "selfish" as being *concerned excessively or exclusively with oneself; seeking or concentrating on one's own advantage, pleasure, or well-being without regard for others.*

Of course, very few of us would consider ourselves Merriam-Webster's definition of selfish. Nevertheless, are we? Is it possible that the overwhelming loads of debt, poor health, broken relationships or moral deficits many of us face are the result of being selfish? At this point, you may be saying to yourself, "I'm not that extreme." Let's be sure. For a moment, close your eyes and ask your spiritual self to speak to you regarding this subject. At this moment, if your spiritual self is revealing a personal truth please do not ignore its voice!

So how did we become unbalanced and sometimes willfully selfish, and more importantly how do we correct this condition? In the computer engineering field, there is a component called a load balancer. Its function is to regulate the flow of electronic information between a host of computers and their centralized mainframe. It does this by giving more important pieces of information higher priority over the less important. Without a load balancer, a computer network would process information slowly and often crash. The load balancer of the soul is our spiritual self. Anything that works to keep us from realizing balance and fulfillment in life is better managed when we develop the awareness of our spiritual self.

Herein resides one of the greatest challenges in life; our spiritual self is often neglected! This challenge exists because our spirits do not cultivate in the same manner as our thoughts and emotions. Our thoughts and emotions develop by doing. In other words, they develop as we go about performing the tasks of daily living; everything we do requires thought and affects our emotions.

Our spiritual self, however, develops most often when we are seemingly doing nothing, at least not in the traditional sense. Spiritual growth usually occurs when we disconnect ourselves from our external world's daily activities. Our spiritual self grows best within *the triangle of the soul* during *quiet time*.

Sadly, most of us are afraid to be quiet and alone with ourselves – yet alone with God! Some of us actually fear the voice within our souls and routinely avoid silence. This is why some people feel they must drive with the radio on when they are alone in the car, turn on the television on even when they are not watching it or are constantly viewing or listening to their handheld device. Consciously or not they are working to avoid *quiet time*.

For a moment, think of someone you love. Because of your love for that person you are more likely to see good in them over the bad, you are always willing to forgive, and will usually go overboard to do things that will increase their happiness. You would not spend every moment of your time condemning and reminding them how undeserving or unworthy they are of your love. The same voice of love and connection to the Creator exists within your soul.

So why does it seem, for many of us, when the external world is quiet the voice within our souls speaks of our failures? The answer is simple. Your voice is addressing a situation that needs attention. That voice is not your enemy, but your connection to the Creator telling you something is keeping you from experiencing more fulfillment in life. Perhaps the reason a painful event continues to replay within your soul is because you have not found healing from it. Perhaps there are situations or activities in your life that are not for your greater good or the people who love and need you, or perhaps you are contributing too much negativity to the Universe. Maybe that replay of past failure is an indication of a *hidden pain* or a warning that you are committing the same mistake. *Most often we avoid the voice from quiet time because it shows us who we really are.*

For a few moments put this book down and sit quietly. Release yourself from any of your to-do lists, reenactments of past experiences or future wishes that may try to swarm your mind. If finding release from the noise in your mind is challenging for you, try using one of the following approaches. For a moment listen to what you are actually thinking about, acknowledge its existence and then tell yourself you are going to put that thought away for a few moments. Another approach is to get a piece of scrap paper, give the idea that's impeding your quiet time a title, write it on your scrap paper and then ball it up and throw it in the garbage.

It may help if you focus on your breathing. Take deep breaths, focus on every inhale and exhale; close your eyes and listen to the sound of your breathing. It may take time, but eventually, the volume of the noises in your head will start to fade. Before you know it, you will begin to hear the voice of your spirit.

During your *quiet time,* ask for guidance on what you need to address. If past failures or pain comes to you, don't resist that voice. Instead, ask for wisdom and guidance on how you need to deal with that situation. The answer may come immediately, or you may only receive one step, or no answer may come to you at that time. If a revelation is revealed to you do not analyze during that time, just accept it as it reveals itself. It may be helpful to record it in your notebook. If nothing comes, continue to cherish your time and by all means, resist the urge to grade the quality of your *quiet time*. Regardless of the foreseeable outcome, every occasion of *quiet time* is a powerfully amazing moment.

Regardless of your current lifestyle or beliefs, your spiritual self is in constant connection with the Creator. Remember it is the essence of God living within you. Therefore, the voice of God is always speaking to you. Negativity, Satan or any other identity of evil you may believe in cannot talk to your spiritual self, but it can speak to your intellectual self, which can then simulate your emotions. Here is the process in more detail. Evil exists in the world; your intellectual self is your connection to the external world. As such, evil can gain access and influence within your soul by means of your thoughts. Minute negative thoughts fueled by our emotion's need to provide ourselves with on-going comfort can produce very powerful reprehensible actions and outcomes. That is why *it is imperative you remain aware of your thoughts and what you allow ourselves to come into contact with*.

## Quiet Time

The fear of being tricked by evil may make some of us hesitant to listen to the voice within our souls. To test the sanctity of the voice you hear during your *quiet time*, take a moment and review what the voice is instructing you. The Creator will never instruct you to take actions that are destructive to you or others. If you find yourself locked into a whirlwind of destructive voices, take a moment and consider its source; it may be the indication of a *hidden pain*. Additionally, resist the urge to deny the voice of your spiritual self solely because the path it is leading you to take will require sacrifice on your part. Oftentimes sacrifice is good for the soul!

In the event, you determine that the voice you hear is purely destructive or negative without reason (beyond a hidden pain), tell that voice it has no place within your soul. Yes, actually say it aloud! Furthermore, once you have rebuked that negative thought from your soul, resist the temptation to allow it to replay itself. You may have to repeat this process several times, but eventually, the volume of that voice should dissipate. If you find that you are unable to quiet those destructive voices, you must reach out for help and share your struggle with someone you love and trust.

During your *quiet time*, if your spiritual self reveals situations that need to be addressed resist the urge to label yourself a bad person. Regardless of the mistakes you made in life, you have divine value. Yes, we are all capable of doing bad things, and we are all guilty of harboring destructive thoughts and feelings, but at our essence, we are not evil. Evil is something that cannot be redeemed; you can. If there were no hope for you to realize more fulfilled life, your spiritual self would not be calling for you to make positive changes. The fact that you are reading these words is proof that the Creator has not given up on you. You have redemptive rights!

Don't be discouraged if initially during your *quiet time* you seem to overwhelmingly hear negative suggestions, that is simply because the longer you've lived and neglected the voice of your spirit, the more issues you need to address. When a situation that needs correction has been revealed to you, don't judge, label nor allow yourself to become trapped into constantly replaying that situation in your mind. Instead, immediately ask for guidance on how to resolve that issue. Remember to write down whatever comes to you. Don't move on to the next situation until you are well on your way to resolving the current one.

As you begin to enhance the balance among your emotional, intellectual, and spiritual self, they will begin to support each other in the manner they were intended. As your spiritual self increases its proportion within the triangle of your soul, your desire to know and understand truth will grow. Additionally, a true awakening of the spirit brings about increased emotional intelligence. As a result, you will begin to have more patience and tolerance for people and situations that easily offended you in the past. You will be more forgiving of others, and more importantly, you will learn how to forgive yourself.

Make experiencing *quiet time* a priority in your life but resist the temptation to make it a task. Make it a time you enjoy; make it truly "me time". If long spans of quiet time do not work for you, try just five minutes or space them out during the day. Your *quiet time* can be any time or place that works best for you. However, it is

## Quiet Time

important that your *quiet time* be somewhere you can be alone and away from as many distractions as possible; a closet full of clothes makes an excellent soundproof room. Do not forget to silence your mobile phone and leave it in another room!

Turning down the volume of our intellectual self in order to hear our spiritual self is a challenge for many of us. Earlier in this chapter, we labeled that voice the "to do" list. That seemingly never-ending list is your intellectual self performing its task of keeping you connected to the external world.

When I first began to dedicate *quiet time*, my thoughts were as a puppy brought home for the first time. My mind ran around aimlessly, at full speed, getting into everything and was completely out of control. It helped me to visualize all of those wild thoughts as such, and which I had to train to sit up straight, be quiet and only move or speak when I gave them permission. Often the list in our minds is geared towards the acquisition of more. If that's the case, you can neutralize that voice by being grateful for the positive things and situation that currently exist in your life. See them as a list, call them out individually and say words of thanksgiving. Then allow your thoughts go free.

When I first started making quiet time a regular part of my life, I also fell asleep a lot. As a result, my spiritual self revealed that I needed to get more sleep and to stop scheduling my quiet time just before bedtime. However, a few minutes of additional *quiet time* before bedtime may influence your dreams to reveal an answer you need. The point to always remember is your *quiet time* is, in fact, your time. Resist the common misconception that your quiet time has to be a pious or arduous task. There are not a long set of rules or steps you must follow. You can sit, stand, kneel; whatever helps you to relax and focus your soul, just try to be in a place that is as quiet or presents natural sounds.

Occasionally during your *quiet time,* you may want to give your soul direction. To accomplish this, simply ask yourself for a solution to a situation you may be experiencing just before you begin your personal *quiet time*. You may not receive an immediate answer, but trust in your divinity, practice patience, and it will be revealed to you at the right time. Do not be afraid of the answer you receive

# Quiet Time

– it may not be the answer you want, but it will be the answer you need. If you have concerns about the answer you receive, ask for confirmation from the Creator. Drawing from my personal experiences; I'm amazed at the number of times I've asked for confirmation to an answer and later opened my Bible to a seemly random page only to read the same answer I received during my *quiet time*. The point is not to look for an answer or confirmation, ask, trust and it will come to you.

Properly interpreting and trusting in the voice we hear from our spiritual self can be unnerving at times and even dangerous if we consider this type of leading too lightly. The primary danger lies in the fact that very often our emotions can seem like the voice of our spirit. Remember your emotional self is more open to receiving guidance from your spiritual self. As such, oftentimes spiritual guidance is initially revealed to us through a feeling rather than a thought. For this reason, confirmation of any guidance you receive is vital, especially when you are new to the process, or when the guidance you receive will bring about radical changes that will impact the lives of those who love and depend on you. If you do not receive a clear confirmation that gives you immediate peace, ask a few people you love and respect how they would handle the situation you are struggling with. Do not tell them what you have heard from your spiritual self upfront; simply ask the hypothetical question and listen.

Dedicating time to hear the voice of your spiritual self is an indescribably rewarding experience. *Quiet time* does more than help you effectively hear the voice of the Creator; it invites God's presence into your soul. You will never be the same! Your focus and personal values will be elevated.

Eventually, your *quiet time* will move beyond addressing situations that are hindering your ability to experiencing more fulfillment in life. Your time will evolve to a level of peace, humility, thanksgiving and the need to help others; even more, and you will have an overabundance of ready strength and wisdom to address challenging situations. Within your *quiet time* you will find the key to one of life's greatest truths: *more fulfillment in life, experiencing harmony with your world, and balance within the soul comes from actively connecting with the Creator.*

## Quiet Time

Right now, make *quiet time*!

# DEALING WITH DEPRESSION

# Dealing with Depression

The definition of depression in this book is not the scientific or clinical diagnosis that requires the assistance of a licensed professional. Depression in this book is a general term. It is that general state of feeling down, out of sync or disconnected with the world; it is an existence we all experience at various points in our lives. This type of general depression is voluntary in nature. As strange as that statement may seem, we actually choose to be depressed. The root of most general depressions stems from the frustration of not finding fulfillment in life. We feel hindered, isolated, trapped, perhaps unloved, or undervalued.

As we develop approaches on how to deal with depression, it is vital we continually and honestly discern if our core causes of depression are not, in fact, overwhelmingly selfish desires rather than a need for genuine life-changing improvements. It is not the intent of this chapter to encourage you to become self-absorbed and certainly not to the extent of hurting the people who love and depend on you. The goal of this chapter is to help you uncover and deal with those situations that are keeping you from experiencing more fulfillment in life; enhance your love relationships and *power to impact the world*.

Are you currently experiencing feelings of depression? What is causing your depression? It may seem there are an intricate number of situations that are causing you to feel depressed, most often the core sources are very short. If you are currently experiencing any level of general depression, take a few moments of *quiet time* and ask your spiritual self to reveal the core sources of your depression. Whatever comes to you write them down. Once again, what is making you feel depressed?

Now consider this; are you depressed because of the existence of that situation or are you depressed because you feel powerless to change it? To expand on this question let us consider a popular source of depression in the modern world, depression over a financial situation. Have you ever been there? Perhaps you are dealing with this situation right now. If so, are you depressed because you think you need more money (its existence), or is it because you can't seem to find a way to obtain or retain more money (ability to change the situation)? Here is another example.

Consider someone who is longing for a meaningful relationship. Is that person depressed because they are not experiencing the relationship they desire, or is it because they feel powerless to change that situation?

Since being overweight is a growing problem in America, let us observe how this situation may cause general depression. Are most people who are depressed about their situation depressed because they are overweight? Or, is it because they feel powerless to do anything meaningful about it? Although the inability to lose excess weight is untrue, some people who are depressed about this situation may have convinced themselves that meaningful change is beyond their ability. They've accepted a feeling of powerlessness, and as a result, a saddled feeling is present within their souls.

No matter how painful or out of control a situation may seem it does not have the power to depress you. General depression is the indication of a disconnection or an imbalance within the triangle of your soul. You are in control of how you feel, think and connect with every situation that occurs in your life. You have the divine authority to control what is allowed to manifest within your soul; therefore, only you can make yourself depressed! *The fuel that furnaces the pain of depression does not come from the external world; it comes from within the triangle of the soul.*

The reason depression has the ability to powerfully impact us is because it can oppress every part of the triangle of the soul. Later in the chapter tilted, *Spiritual Self...More* we will discuss more deeply how symptoms of depression may emanate from our spiritual self, for now we will focus on where most forms of depression reside; our thoughts and emotions.

So, how does the soul deal with depression and find healing? The process is relativity simple; identify both *what* and *why* a depressing situation exists and then take action steps. Let's expand on this concept. A vital step in the process is to honestly and clearly identify *what* is causing your intellectual self to be locked into a pattern of constantly replaying a seemingly depressing situation. An equally important part of the process is allowing your emotional self to reveal *why* a situation is causing you the feeling of depression. The final step is to empower yourself by taking actions aimed directly at addressing that seemingly depressing situation.

Let's observe the process in the context of the overweight person. *What* is making them depressed is the idea that they are in an undesired situation. The reason *why* they feel depressed is because they feel that they can do very little to change the situation. They feel powerless both intellectually and emotionally concerning that situation.

Here is an alternate example. Think about the person who lost their job. The fact they are unemployed is *what* is causing them experience depression about that situation. The reason *why* they are experiencing feelings of depression is due to the loss of emotional comfort caused by the realities of an uncertain financial future and the unwanted challenge of searching for a new job.

Now that we understand the difference between what and why we experience depression, let's get to work dealing with depression within your soul and develop self-empowering actions that will eliminate that state of being. If you are not currently experiencing any form of depression, continue reading this chapter, as it will help you cope with those situations when they arise in the future. To follow along with this process, you will need to go to the *Dealing with Depression* section of your Triangle of the Soul: Support Book or you can use your notepad.

Take a few moments of *quiet time* and write down in as few words as possible; *what* situation is making you feel depressed. Don't analyze the situation or your feelings toward it – just write. Now, review what you have written. If you wrote down more than one situation, do you see a commonality among them? If not, then they are separate situations and need be addressed separately. Summarize whichever statements that have common themes together; this is your "what statement".

Choose whichever situation you would like to work on first. Then for a few moments allow your soul to reveal *why* you are depressed about that situation. Simply ask yourself, "Why is this situation depressing me?" As you write don't be afraid of what you uncover, resist the need to justify yourself, nor be politically correct or even nice; be brazenly honest. Give this some time and be sure to list everything that comes to you. When you are satisfied that you have uncovered every aspect of this situation take a moment and review your list and once again look to combine commonalities. Except for this time, you will keep whatever remains on the list, these are your "why statements".

We have learned earlier that general depression is a voluntary decision. Therefore, the external world is not the primary source of your depression: you are! Accepting this truth, review your "why statements" and draw a line through any items that highlight another person as the primary source of your depression. Yes, the pain they contribute to that situation is real. However, you cannot change the way another person chooses to interact with you outside the confines of the law. Since you cannot change them and they are not the primary source of our general depression: they don't matter! So cross all the items attributed to them off your list.

*Although we can influence how other people perceive us, we cannot make them love, like or appreciate us more than they are willing.* Understanding, accepting and then taking proper actions regarding this truth will free you from untold amounts of pain and perhaps release you from most of your depressed feelings. Always remember, you cannot control someone's feelings, but you have supreme control of your own. Other people can influence your feelings, but you are the captain of the ship of your soul. You may love that person or be inexplicably attached to a situation that is triggering those feelings of depression in your life, but they do not have authority over your soul. Not even God Almighty will force a feeling you are willing to accept. Certainly, the people or situations that are triggering the feelings of depression in your life are not greater than God!

Let's move forward. Select one of the "why statements" you did not cross out and place a laser focus on that statement. A depressing situation presents two simultaneous experiences within your soul. What you think about that statement is your intellectual self in action and why you feel a certain way about that statement is your emotional self. For example, a person can think losing weight is too hard and can also feel defeated because of past experiences. Now review one of your "why statements", ask yourself, "What do I *think* about that statement and then how does it make me *feel*?"

## Dealing with Depression

As humans, we are capable of maintaining ideas defined in this book as surface truths. A *surface truth* is something that seems to be true until further examination. A surface truth may be when someone says, "It's impossible for me to save money." However, when that person further examines their personal spending habits, they may uncover areas upon which they are needlessly spending money; such as, eating out too often, overindulgent shopping or entertainment. Once they've drilled down beyond the *surface truth* they discovered, it is not impossible to save money; the truth is they have chosen to maintain habits that require the money they could have been saving.

For moment ask yourself if any of your "why statements" are in fact surface truths. If they are, a solution to addressing those situations will come to you quickly, note them and immediately begin adjusting your lifestyle accordingly. Then remove those items from your list because they are not at the core of your general depression. Remember they are quick fixes.

Let's deal more deeply with the reaming "why statements" on your list. Since your intellectual self predominately interprets all situations from a logical perspective, we will uncover what you think about one of your "why statements" from a logical perspective. This is achieved by simply asking, "What do I need to do to change my situation?" Write down whatever comes to you. Yes, it's that simple. Here's why. Your intellectual self is constantly working to find the best solutions towards maintaining your material fulfillment in life, even while you are asleep. Since it is always at work, it usually has a logical answer to every situation in your life. Your intellectual self cannot restrain itself from devising an answer to any question. If it doesn't have a ready answer for you, it will begin working on one immediately after you ask the question.

We often discount the logical answers our intellectual self provides us because they seem too simple or because we do not like them. Let's go back to our overweight friend. Their intellectual self may have been telling them for some time that the key to losing weight is making better eating choices and exercising regularly. Although execution of the solution may seem difficult the logical answer is simple. Our intellectual self seldom changes the solutions to a situation unless a more logical solution is obtained through increased knowledge. As you ask your intellectual self for solutions to the depressing situations in your life, it is very likely you have heard them before; this time take heed!

Unlike your thoughts, your feelings are rarely surface truths. In other words, every feeling you experience is real. We have learned from the chapter titled, *Emotional Self* that feelings can be manipulated, however, if we are truly experiencing general depression (as opposed to clinical depression); your feelings about a depressing situation are real. Furthermore, your emotional self is clearly aware of how that situation is affecting your soul, as such you will be able to clearly identify, and easily articulate the problem. Usually, the resistance we experience when connecting emotionally to a depressing situation is because it causes pain; not because we are unable to identify it. Remember one of our emotional self's main functions is to maintain comfort within the soul; even if it involves avoiding the pain of a situation that is causing us to feel depressed.

## Dealing with Depression

The key to dealing with the feeling of depression within your emotional self is to *feel differently*. Again, I know that sounds too simple and it is. Here is an illustration. You can fill a balloon with breaths of air or helium. Both gases will cause the balloon to expand, but only one will cause it to rise. Visualize your emotions as that balloon. Your emotions can be filled with useless negative information that causes it to fall to the ground or powerful positive feelings that will raise it to the heavens.

So how do we change our feelings, especially about a debilitating situation that is causing general depression? Remember, general depression arises when we feel that we are not experiencing some level of fulfillment in life. We may feel hindered, hopeless or even powerless to change our situation. As such, the most powerful thing we can do is take action! The actions you take may not need to be radical, but they must be deliberate, self-aware, and constructive self-empowering actions.

Your self-empowering actions become even more powerful when you announce them while you are performing them. Here are a few examples. Each time our overweight friend exercises or makes better eating choices, they could say, "At this moment I am exercising or taking a better eating choice so I can look like the person I desire." The people with financial challenges who put themselves on a strict shopping and entertainment budget may say something like "I am not going to waste my money on that purchase, so I can have money to save and apply to more important items."

This is such a powerful key let us read a few more examples. "I am taking this night class so I can earn a degree and get a better job." "I am making this personal effort to be a better spouse, parent, friend so I can have better relationships." Do you feel the power in these statements? It is impossible to continue to feel overwhelmingly depressed about your situation when you know you are actively working towards addressing them. It all starts with the key, you! You have to make yourself feel differently about your situation; empower yourself.

Once again review your "why statements", but this time ask the Creator to reveal self-empowering action steps that can address each of them. Write down whatever comes to you and start doing them today; right now! Remember your self-empowering action steps do not have to be complicated neither do they need to be announced to the world. They can be simple small changes; steps you can do regularly.

The larger a hot air balloon is, the longer it will take to rise off the ground; makes sense. Some of your feelings of general depression may change faster than others, that's okay. Don't give up! Just keep reminding yourself that each time you take the self-empowering action you are rising; floating away from those feelings of depression and towards finding more fulfillment in life.

You have the divine ability to overcome all situations that are causing you to experience general depression. Remember, general depression stems from the frustration we feel when we are not experiencing our divine order of fulfillment in life. Regardless of how unfair or out of control situations in your life may seem, accept the fact that you have the divine rights to a fulfilled life. Beware, if your self-empowering steps will harm the people who truly love, care and depend on you do not pursue them. In fact, in those situations, it is prudent to honestly and intensely explore why your core feelings of depression stem from selfishness rather than a divine desire to find more fulfillment in life.

*Special note:*

*Although the information we just read about in this chapter can be applied to situations in life that are causing you to feel "general depression", other forms of clinical depression require additional help. Ongoing anxiety, an inability to function in society, panic attacks, uncontrollable impulsiveness actions or ongoing thoughts of causing harm to yourself or others must be shared with a licensed qualified professional. In conjunction with help from those sources, perhaps this book can serve as an additional tool to assist you in your healing.*

Led by the Spirit

We now know that within the *triangle of the soul*, our greatest connection to God is through our spiritual self. Through this connection, we receive God's influence, wisdom, and direction for our lives. Now let us dig deeper into how to better connect with our spiritual self and learn how to follow its lead.

I enjoy visiting public zoos. I think most of them provide a great service for humans, and the many animals they keep. However, I often feel a little sad for the caged large birds. Although they usually look well fed and healthy, I cannot help thinking how much they desire to fully extend their wings and fly away. Yes, their basic needs are met, but they were created to do more. Like our well-cared-for animal friends at the zoo, most of our basic needs are met. But are we soaring in our greatness?

You are created to do more than just let life happen, beg or hope for the best. You are here to contribute your talents and gifts to the world! No other person thinks, feels, or experiences God and the world like you, therefore; no other person can impact the world like you. You have a divine purpose. Your divine purpose is not a mystical or a difficult thing to understand. Your divine purpose or purposes are the gifts and talents which were placed within your soul at your creation. Since they were given to you by the Creator and your spiritual self is well aware of them. As such, your spiritual self is constantly working to lead you towards fulfilling your divine purpose.

The question we must ask ourselves is, "Are we following the leading of our spiritual self and allowing it to contribute our divinity to the world?" Right now, say these words aloud, "Am I living the kind of life I was created to have, am I contributing my divinity, my uniqueness?" It is impossible to neglect the leading of your spiritual self and find more fulfillment in life.

Of course, your spiritual self will never lead you to abandon responsibilities for your actions or hurt the people who love and depend on you. Nevertheless, it would be a tragedy to have a life that does not contribute the divine uniqueness or gifts within your soul in some way. The triangle of your soul has the fingerprint of the Creator impressed on it, which means you inherently have the ability and power to create. In fact, you created the overall outcome of your current situations in life. This may be a difficult truth to accept on some levels, nevertheless, it is true.

Your self-image, level of intelligence, emotional strength, personal relationships, spiritual awareness, personal living space and whatever is connected to you is the result of your actions – they are your creations. Take a moment and focus on accepting the fact that you are a creator. Essentially, you created your world. Furthermore, there is a direct correlation to the level of fulfillment in life you are currently experiencing to the intensity you have followed the leading of your spirit during your creation process.

You were created to enjoy and experience your life to its fullest, and your spiritual self is here to lead you. All voluntary actions you take that hinder you from following your spiritual self's leading will cause pain and sickness within the soul; the presence of depression. It is an undeniable truth that we must engage in activities that do not seem to enhance our divinity. Perhaps this is an added meaning to the concept of being born into sin.

At this point, you may be asking, "How do I know if I am following the leading of my spirit?" This question can be answered with one word, peace. When we take actions that are contrary to the leading of our spiritual self, the triangle of our soul will not allow us to experience peace; we sense something is wrong. Your spiritual self is in constant connection with the Divine and as such is continually at work within your soul trying to lead you towards activities that will enhance your peace.

Peace is not dependent upon external factors; it is an internal state of calmness, unity, security, and acceptance. Situations of pain may abound in your external world while peace thrives within your soul. A key to finding more fulfillment in life is *understanding that only you and your connection to the Creator can establish your peace.*

More deeply, to experience peace within your soul you cannot be the source of pain in others. Take a few moments of *quiet time* and ask your spiritual self if you are contributing to the pain of others or yourself. If your spirit has revealed any faults on your behalf resist the need to dwell on them. Instead, ask the Creator to give you directions on how to eliminate that evil. While you are receiving guidance, take notes and then act quickly. Delayed actions may give your emotions an opportunity to convince you to stay comfortable and not deal with that conflict.

As we contemplate how we can increase our ability to follow the leading from our spirit, another question to ask is, "How do I know if the instructions I'm receiving are coming from my spiritual self?" Again the answer is inherently within you; simply ask yourself "Is this guidance for the greater good?" Your spiritual self will not lead towards actions that will intentionally cause pain into the lives of other souls. However, as a result of following its leadership, the situations in your life will change.

The clarity of the guidance you receive is dependent upon the condition and balance within the triangle of your soul. A person who seems to routinely make wrong choices, is constantly indecisive or unclear of their place in this world, such a person is not following the leading of their spirit. If you desire greater clarity for your life, then you must spend more *quiet time* developing the voice of your spiritual self and your connection to the Divine.

A major premise of this book is built upon finding more fulfillment in life; however, we have refrained from defining fulfillment in life on purpose. That's because the definition is different for each of us. Even more, our personal definition of fulfillment changes as we experience life. For some, fulfillment in life seems elusive because they erroneously identified it by its symptoms rather than its true existence. For example, happiness is a symptom of having more fulfillment in life, but peace is fulfillment in life. Happiness is a temporary state we experience when the needs of our intellectual and/or emotional self are reasonably met. Happiness is real and needed in life; however, it is meant to be temporary. *The on-going pursuit of any temporary experience will hinder your ability to find more fulfillment in life.*

Fulfillment in life is not defined by your level of happiness, but your level of peace. An ultimate key to finding more fulfillment in life is understanding that *God is much more concerned about the level of peace in your life opposed to your happiness.* Your spiritual self will not always lead you to take actions that will make you happy. This may be a difficult concept to accept, but it is radically true. Sometimes we deny the leading of our spiritual self when it doesn't seem to be leading us towards actions that will immediately increase our happiness. As a result, we are unable to experience a complete relationship with the Creator; we are afraid of losing those temporary moments of happiness or comfort. Have you ever lost faith regarding a situation because it did not immediately feed your happiness?

Within the triangle of your soul, your spirit's connection to God is constant. The knowledge or knowing of God has no boundaries; everything has the essence of God. As such, a part of your soul is connected to everything made by God. In other words, the knowing of everything is available to you through your spiritual self, especially as it pertains to you and your ability to find more fulfillment in life.

Being led by the spirit may be challenging at times because it defies logic. Your spiritual self often receives instructions on a level of knowledge that defies the major decision maker within the soul, your intellect. Your intellectual self is designed to reject any information or instructions it cannot understand. However, through studying spiritual teachings, its faith or ability to accept guidance from your spiritual self can improve. This is why it is said that faith comes by hearing. Hearing is primarily an intellectual function.

Earlier we learned, one of the primary functions of our emotional self is to maintain a certain level of comfort within the soul, as such, it is prone to lead us toward activities that are self-serving. The voice of our spiritual self is usually the lowest within the soul, it seldom speaks many words, and it usually reveals itself as a feeling or an undefinable knowing. Additionally, its leadership rarely reveals a definitive outcome that will result in greater comfort (happiness). As such, our emotions have the propensity to diminish or augment its guidance or even disguise and present itself as our spiritual self.

# Led by the Spirit

Before you accept any guidance that seems to be spiritual put it on trial. In other words, try the spirit by the spirit. Remember the one you can use is to simply ask, "Is this thing I am being led to do for the greater good?" If you are still unsure, place those instructions to the side, engage in some *quiet time*, reevaluate the balance within your soul, and be patient. Eventually, the answer will reveal itself. Yes, there will be occasions when the leading of your spirit may not seem logical, scary and may not give you foreseeable happiness, but it will speak to your *power to impact the world*. It will speak to your peace, to your knowing and it will lead you down the path to more fulfillment in life.

# Uncovering Hidden Pains

## Uncovering Hidden Pains

Throughout our journey of life, the state of our intellectual and emotional selves is continually being developed and changed by our experiences. Our intellect learns new ways of understanding life's experiences, while our emotional self interprets their impact on our personal comfort. Whether we are aware of it or not, absolutely every moment of our lives is remembered and interpreted. This never-ending process continues even while we sleep.

Whether positive or negative every experience in life is processed for use within the soul. Pleasurable or rewarding experiences encourage us to grow towards and peruse them more deeply, while painful situations repel us. However, some painful experiences extend beyond our personal definitions of reasonable mishaps and are too difficult for our souls to process. In a desperate attempt to keep us from being completely overtaken by the trauma of those experiences, our intellectual and emotional selves store those events away with the intention of dealing with them later.

## Uncovering Hidden Pains

As a short-term approach, this process works to our benefit. However, when we store those pains away too long, dangerous conditions begin to develop. Our emotional self begins to dread reliving those experiences and out of fear keep us from dealing with them. In an attempt to logically process painfully illogical events and make them more palatable, our intellectual self may distort or cause us to forget some of the facts of those events.

As a result of these two processes fear and a distorted view of our world finds a place within the triangle of the soul; they become *hidden pains*. When something is hidden, it takes up space and interacts with the environment, although its presence may not be known; it does exist. It is reasonable to assume that everyone has experienced at least one particularly painful event that was too difficult to quickly overcome and has become a *hidden pain*.

We may not be able to recall the event or may have become somewhat numb to its sting. Some of us have become reluctant experts at suppressing our pains and so, we try our best to ignore them. Nevertheless, they still exist and are active open wounds in our souls.

## Uncovering Hidden Pains

Most unreasonable reactions to life's challenges originate from *hidden pains*. Some of these expressions are dangerous and show themselves in violent or aggressive manners; while others seem innocent but are equally caustic. Practically all fears, addictions, persistent negativities, self-destructive behaviors, acts of cruelty, intolerance, overwhelmingly selfish behaviors, vanity, uncontrollable anger, envy, the list goes on, are all outcomes of *hidden pains.*

When we hold on to a *hidden pain* too long, it becomes a part of our personality. Perhaps you know someone who has a hidden pain within their soul. It may be that person learned that being mean or hard is simply a part of their personality or what they had to become to survive. They may be someone who feels nobody understands their challenges in life or nobody's life is as difficult as theirs. Perhaps, they feel they were not created to experience fulfillment in life. A very common *hidden pain* in the western world is the concept that success through the attainment of possessions and notable accomplishments brings happiness. Sadly this concept is so pervasive that many people are unaware they hold onto this pain. What is your *hidden pain*?

For a moment, visualize a small child who is riding a tricycle that has the rubber linings removed from the front wheel. With effort (more than should be required), the child is able to ride the tricycle, but due to its broken condition, the child cannot steer it properly. The experience of riding the tricycle is not fun; the child often falls and hurts themselves and sometimes others. Now, envision you are that child riding throughout your life's journey. Are all three of your wheels (the triangle of the soul) in good condition? Does the daily activity of living seem to be harder than it should? Do you feel lucky if you have a "good day"? Are there situations in your life that are out of control or are you dealing with a lot of stress?

The child in our story might or might not have been aware a wheel on the bike was impaired. Whatever the case the overwhelming desire or pressure to ride overshadowed the will to address the situation. If they were aware, most likely they lacked the knowledge on how to repair their situation, were afraid or simply gave up on the idea of fixing the problem and decided to ride through with the pain. In other words, they decided to hide the pain and ride on with a broken life.

So how do we find something that's been hidden for so long a time it that it became a part of our character? The answer is simple; truth. Truth is impartial and uncompromising. Truth is indiscriminate towards who uses it and exists whether we choose to acknowledge it or not; truth exists on its own. Only truth has the ability to expose *hidden pains* and the power to set us free. When we understand and accept the truth about a painful event, it can no longer remain hidden within *the triangle of the soul.*

Most often hidden pains cloak themselves from being discovered by casting blame. Blame is a device used by our emotional self to provide us with some sort of comfort. It may be difficult for some of us to admit, but often there is an uneasy comfort in believing someone else is the cause of our imbalance. Blame is also notorious for its ability to coax our intellectual self into distorting the truth of experiences. Ultimately, blame distracts us away from uncovering the hidden pains within our souls.

## Uncovering Hidden Pains

The only way to break through blame's cloak surrounding a *hidden pain* is to take full responsibility for your actions regarding that painful event. Taking full responsibility is achieved when you take to eliminate any possibility of opting out. Opting out may sound something like this: "I knew it wasn't the right thing to do, but..." or "The only reason I did that is because...."

Is there an activity you are currently engaging in that your spiritual self is telling you is not good for you, but instead of following its guidance you are using options to justify your actions? Worse, is there a *hidden pain* influencing your soul to sustain this destructive behavior?

Your spiritual self is your connection to the Creator. As such, your spirit only knows the truth; it exists to enhance balance within your soul and works endlessly to help you find more fulfillment in life. Therefore, you must involve your spiritual self to help guide you through the process of uncovering, overcoming, and healing your soul from *hidden pains.*

The first step towards uncovering hidden pains is establishing *quiet time* and to ask yourself *why*; "Why do I maintain habits, thoughts, or feelings that I know are not for my greater good...what happened to me?" Most likely the first response you will receive will be a replay of painful experiences that were caused by another person. This response is valid, however, it is causing you to hide and by default hold onto the pain of that experience. Unfortunately, many of us stay on this level because it justifies our actions. This is blame in disguise. You must go deeper. You must go beyond the actions of others and to the place you accepted that painful situation into your soul. Remember your intellectual self records and the emotional self feels every moment that impacts your life, so truest form of that pain situation can be uncovered.

Go deeper. Allow your spiritual self to guide your thoughts and emotions to show you the pains that have been plaguing your soul. It's there, be patient, honest with yourself and listen. If the voice from your spiritual self is unclear perhaps you are spending too much energy trying to replay every detail surrounding that past situation. Free yourself from the details and focus on how that painful event makes you *feel* right now.

## Uncovering Hidden Pains

As your spiritual self guides you to revelations allow yourself to identify that pain in one word. Now, openly and honestly say that one word that has been torturing your soul. Say it aloud! Hear yourself say it. Accept the fact that this pain is real and inside you. That word represents everything your *hidden pain* has grown into; it is your *hidden pain*.

If you are confident that you have uncovered at least one of your hidden pains, then feel free to move on to the next chapter titled, *Healing from Hidden Pains*. If you are not satisfied with your results, please continue reading.

In some cases the reason why you maintain habits or activities that are for your greater good may seem to be unclear. In other words, you are telling yourself you don't know why you maintain destructive actions. Your spiritual self is connected to the all-knowing God, therefore, that response is most likely invalid or more covered than you realize. Take another step, ask yourself "What event in my life am I deeply ashamed or afraid to mention? Is there a painful secret I am keeping within my soul?"

## Uncovering Hidden Pains

It is estimated that over one hundred seven billion people have lived on earth to this point. Although your painful event was intense and real, it is not unique.

You can uncover and find healing from that pain. Take solace in the fact that since you began reading this book, the triangle of your soul has grown, and so has your relationship with the Creator. You are stronger, more balanced, aware and equipped with the tools you need to have more fulfillment in life. It's time to uncover those hidden pain and be healed.

If you decide a *hidden pain* is too difficult for you to uncover on your own share your struggle with someone you love and trust, and possibly a licensed professional who is skilled at helping people deal with their situations.

*Hidden pains can only be uncovered when we accept the absolute truth regarding a situation.* In order to accomplish this task, you must resist the temptation to place blame and on some level re-experience some of the worst moments of your life. Nevertheless, the rewards of intense peace, freedom from pain and finding more fulfillment in life are worth the effort.

## Uncovering Hidden Pains

You are stronger than you have ever been in life. Dedicate yourself to spending *quiet time* to truly uncover what's been causing pain within your soul. You can do it. You will prevail! In our next chapter entitled *Healing from Hidden Pains*, we will develop action steps that will support you on your journey to finding more fulfillment in life.

# Healing from Hidden Pains

Before we learn more about the steps that will bring about *healing from hidden pains*, we may need to change our understanding of pain. Pain in any form is a signal that something is wrong and needs attention. For example, the pain of an upset stomach, muscles, joints or a headache is all a signal that your body is not functioning properly and is in need of help. The same concept applies to hidden pains within the triangle of the soul. Although pain's presence within the soul and the events that caused it are traumatic, it serves the vital purpose of informing you something is wrong within. As we delve into this chapter keep the idea that your *hidden pain* is not the problem but the indicator, in other words, your *hidden pain* exists to serve you, to expose where you need help.

When a very painful event occurs, *the triangle of the soul* goes into overdrive in an attempt to deal with the situation. Since your emotions and intellect are the parts of your soul that are most affected by that painful event, they take lead roles in dealing with it. Many of our hidden pains originate from a perceived misapplication of fairness. Most of us generally agree upon what is fair, however, everyone measures and identifies with fairness differently. Moreover, our perception of fairness is governed by the condition of our souls.

An imbalanced soul that is more led by its intellectual self will be more connected to material possessions and tend to measure fairness by physical possessions or situations. A person who is overly connected with their emotional self will define the fairness of a situation by how much comfort it provides. Our spiritual self does not consider fairness in any way; it only focuses on what is and what is true.

Fairness is our conceptual measurement of the truths or a form of logic. We use these self-developed forms or logic or ideas of fairness to measure our significance in the world. When the outcome from a painful event is determined to be unfair, *the triangle of the soul's* stability is disrupted. This is especially true when we are powerless to influence the outcome of that situation that seemed unfair. During many of these situations, our intellectual self will replay that event many times in an attempt to make sense of that painful experience. It is trying to make an unfair event seem logical or fair and therefore acceptable.

Have you ever had a painful experience that you just couldn't seem to stop thinking about? Most likely, that event did not fit into your definition of fairness. When this process is continually replayed and reinforced it becomes a habit. Eventually, that habit of negative thinking becomes a part of how we understand and connect to the external world.

The most effective way to deal with habitually negative thoughts caused by a painful event is to forgive. Remember, the reason our thoughts become locked into replaying these painful events is because it is trying to make sense of the situation; it is trying to find redemption from the pain. Depending on the condition of our souls some of us may try to force redemption from a painful event by the use of revenge or manipulation, some allow pain to devolve into resentment. Whichever the case, these actions can push our souls into a yearning for an outcome that will most likely never happen, nor free us from our hidden pains. *Forgiveness is the only liberator from hidden pains within the triangle of the soul.*

One of the primary functions of our emotional self is to provide our soul with some sort of comfort; it seeks to avoid pain with little regard for its outcome. When we allow our emotional self to take the lead role in dealing with hidden pains oftentimes it inadvertently multiplies pain; first by leading us into making irrational decisions that reinforce our painful situations, next by causing pain or adding to pain in others.

To heal from hidden pains, we need to employ all three parts of our soul. Frist, we will need our spiritual self to reveal the truth. Truth allows our intellect make sense of painful events and it enables our emotions to clearly interpret how those events caused us pain and how we may have hurt others.

In the previous chapter titled, *Uncovering Hidden Pains* we learned that most hidden pains could be identified in a few words. Even more, those words can be narrowed to just one word. If you haven't done so, take a few moments of *quiet time* and narrow the words that identify your hidden pain into just one. That word is the identity or label you've given that particular pain, it is its source of power, and it uses that power to exist and affect the triangle of your soul.

The process we are about to follow to find *healing from hidden pains* works best when we deal with one event at a time. You may have endured several painful events in your life, and every one of them will require attention. However, at this point whichever event came to you first while in the previous chapter is most likely the first situation you need to find healing from.

You will need your notebook or your Triangle of the Soul: Support Sheet to complete the following exercise. Imagine you are in a movie theater and playing on the screen is the painful event you just identified. Instead of being a participant of that painful event you are in the theater watching that event transpire on-screen. As the events of the movie unfold, what feelings are you experiencing? List whatever best describes your feelings. Was the outcome that unfolded on-screen fair? What emotions do you feel towards the characters who participated in the events that hurt the main character of the movie (you)? Write down the names of those people and the emotions you feel towards them. Did the main character pay an unfair price as a result of those events? If yes, what price did they pay? Finally, ask yourself, "Why does the memory of that event still cause me pain?" Take your time and allow your spiritual self to help you uncover the truth to these questions.

The act of releasing yourself and others from past pains is called forgiveness. *A vital step towards healing is realized when you declare your forgiveness of the people who caused you pain.* This step must be taken even if that person has not asked for forgiveness, is unaware, or even denies their level of involvement in your pain. Forgiveness is necessary for your personal healing. Even if you feel that person is not worthy of your forgiveness. *A key to finding more fulfillment in life is understanding that we forgive those who hurt us for our benefit, not theirs; forgiveness is self-serving.* Un-forgiveness fortifies the power of a *hidden pain* and its ability to hold us captive to past painful events. *Healing within the triangle of the soul only comes to those who are free.* Today is your day to be set free from your past; today you will be healed!

Once again, unless you forgive others who caused you pains you will never receive healing from those hurtful events. Your personal healing from hidden pain is all that matters. As a creature made in the image of God, you have the divine power to forgive others even those you feel are unworthy. It is the same power the Almighty applies to forgive and accept your shortcomings.

Use the process outlined in the next sentence to individually declare your divine power to forgive every person who caused you pain during a particular event. The process will sound something like this; "(say their full name) I declare my divine power to forgive you for (insert the painful event they contributed to here). I release you from your ability to continue to cause me pain and imbalance in my soul. I forgive you. I release you. I wish you well."

Once you have said these words aloud, cross that person's name off your sheet. Repeat this process until you have individually named and forgiven every person who has caused you pain during that particular event.

After you've declared your divine right to forgive all of the people who caused you pain it is time to request forgiveness from the Creator, especially if God is one of the characters in your movie with whom you are angry. For some, the idea of being angry with God may not seem evident or we may choose to deny it. Most of us reading this book believe there is an ultimate power, energy or God that created and governs our reality. Additionally, we believe God has a divine purpose of love and goodness for all of us; fulfillment in life. As such, when painful events occur, sometimes we question God's love or ability to care for us. We question God's fairness and say things such as "Does God really care?" or "Does God really exist?" or "Why is this happening to me?" In those moments, your emotional self is saying painful events aren't supposed to happen to you because God is supposed to protect you. While your intellectual self is saying, "God didn't, the Creator failed me." Do you have a *hidden pain* against the Creator?

In the identity of a father, God is just, loving, understanding and faithful to forgive us of all our misdoings, even anger against the Divine. God forgives you simply because you ask for it.

Additionally, it is critically important you ask forgiveness of the Creator even if you were an innocent recipient of the event that caused you pain. Here is why. Regardless of your level of fault regarding a painful event on some level, you generated negative energy towards God's divine creation. The presence of that negativity will cause a level of separation between you and the Creator. Remember, forgiveness is self-serving.

Whenever your physical body suffers a wound, it takes time to heal; so does *the triangle of the soul*. Although the wounds that caused you pain have been uncovered and treated, that area of your soul may be tender and sore for a while. The more deeply entrenched and severe the event that caused you pain, the longer it will take to heal. For some time you may have to change the dressing over your pain by reminding yourself that you have received healing over that situation; you've forgiven those who hurt you, you've forgiven yourself and the Creator. Allow the triangle of your soul to move you through the process; one moment at a time on your way to finding more fulfillment in life.

# HEALER OF HIDDEN PAINS

Earlier you spoke the words of forgiveness that released others from the pain they caused you. Now it is time for you to offer healing to the people you hurt. For a moment, refocus on one of the events from which you gained healing. Now ask yourself, "Whom do I need to ask to forgive me?" Immediately, your spiritual self will show the face of each person you need to ask forgiveness (they may be the same people you identified previously as hurting you).

Here is a critical warning! At this point, your emotional self may be going into overdrive to convince you to maintain your current state of comfort by reinforcing the need to place blame. It may incite fear or shame to force you to stay within your current level of comfort. Your emotions may try to convince your intellectual self that those people are not worthy or may not receive your words of forgiveness. Your intellect may recall how much you did not deserve the treatment you received; it may even deduce they should be requesting forgiveness from you instead.

Resist these temptations; focus on your goal of achieving greater balance and healing within your soul. As stated earlier, the act of forgiving is a self-serving, especially when you must ask forgiveness from the unforgiving.

The ability to openly request forgiveness from someone whom you feel does not deserve it or who remains unforgiving requires understanding. This level of understanding is powerful beyond measure; it enhances the flow or favor of God into your life. Here is the understanding. A part of the triangle of every soul is the essence of the Creator, our spiritual self. It is impossible to fully experience the presence of the Creator while you maintain negative energy against another soul; God's essence.

You are not responsible for a person's willingness to accept your forgiveness. Your only responsibility is to not cast blame, be sincere, honest, and specific when you request forgiveness. How they receive your request is literally a matter between them and God. Again, you do not need them to forgive you; you only need to ask for it.

The process of requesting forgiveness from someone whom you caused pain is the same as illustrated earlier; call the person by name, identify the painful event and directly ask that person to forgive you, except this time you are doing it in person. Since these people are most likely not accessible to you at this moment, write down each person's name and set a target date of when you will personally ask for their forgiveness, then cross that person's name off your list after you have met with them.

If that person is available right now, put down this book, go to them, and ask for forgiveness for causing them pain for a specific event. If those people have passed away, hold a fond memory of them in your soul and then aloud ask them to forgive you. The act of forgiving or requesting forgiveness from another person is an amazingly self-empowering step towards receiving healing from hidden pains; it is something you must do.

There may be some situations you will need to help uncovering and addressing hidden pains. While it is always prudent to reach out for help when needed, be very careful of whom you allow to help assist you in dealing with your hidden pains. Remember, they may have hidden pains as well. If you find yourself unable to clearly uncover a hidden pain or action steps for healing without incorporating the influence of someone else, you have become too dependent on that person(s). You are in danger!

You are a divine creation of God; you were not designed to rely on the external world to balance the triangle of your soul. When we rely too heavily on the guidance of others to provide us with balance and direction within our souls, we are giving them power over our lives. History is full with people who have harmed themselves and others through the misuse of this power. The only true authority that can thoroughly empower us to uncover and receive healing from hidden pains is the Creator. During your *quiet time* of uncovering hidden pains, utilize your spiritual self's ongoing connection with the Creator for help and guidance. Reaching out to God is not a complicated or mysterious process; you were born with this ability. You don't have to belong to a particular group or organization to speak to God. The Creator of your soul knows your voice and understands your situation far better than you can explain it, so just talk.

If you are currently incorporating the help of a qualified licensed professional and/or using prescribed medicines to help you cope with the pains hidden within your soul, it is NOT in your best interest to abruptly discontinue their support. However, your ultimate goal should be to become able to uncover your hidden pains and receive healing primarily with the help of the Creator. This is not to diminish the role and tremendous support you can receive from professionals and people who truly love you. We are all created with the capacity to help each other. However, relying on tonics to alter your intellectual and emotional selves is counter to the divine design of the Creator.

Remember, realization and acceptance of the truth, humility, *quiet time* with God, and forgiveness will bring about your healing from all of the hidden pains within *the triangle of the soul*.

## SPIRITUAL SELF....MORE

The primary role of our spiritual self is to enable us to connect with the Creator. This connection spans beyond our awesome ability to talk to God; it also enables God to talk to us. This connection makes us the most powerful beings in our reality. Although we use our thoughts and emotions to express our adoration for God, God is a spirit; therefore, we can only wholly worship God with our spiritual self (which can occur without outward expressions).

Our spiritual self is the Creator's fingerprints that were left on our souls during birth, some call it the breath of life. In other words, our spiritual self is the essence of God living within us. This divine essence makes it possible for us to experience and appreciate all of the things that are naturally beautiful in this world.

*Our spiritual self is the orchestrator of balance and peace within the soul and is the keeper of all our keys to fulfillment in life.* Through its connection to God it empowers us to forgive past offenses, seek the greater good, unites us in alliances of love and peace, and endows us with the ability to sacrifice.

Our spiritual self connects us to a reality that usually cannot be seen or controlled in the tangible, logical world; therefore, our intellect is often our spirit's greatest rival. However, the two were not created to compete against each other but are designed to work together to expand wisdom. As we discussed earlier, our intellectual self's role is to keep us connected to the physical world; as such, it also provides us with the means to coordinate the influences of our emotional and spiritual selves with the world.

This coordination is recognizable when we perform tasks that seem to extend beyond our normal abilities; such as remarkable artistic expressions, innovative scientific developments, or the realization of life-changing revelations. The greatest example of our ability to coordinate the power of the soul is effectual faith. Faith is an actual substance; it is the proof of the existence of something that is currently unrealized; faith is hoping for the manifestation of a future outcome.

We need our intellectual and spiritual selves to give faith life. Faith depends on our spiritual self to influence our thoughts to take actions towards supporting a currently nonexistent outcome. We call this belief. Conversely, we need our intellect to identify our needs, which in turn are communicated to the Creator through our spirit.

When we experience intense connections to God, our emotions are more likely to respond to it over our thoughts. Praying is the process whereby we influence the power of God. We will discuss this process in more details in the chapter entitled, *Power of Faith.*

As we mentioned earlier, our spirit is the Creator's fingerprints on our soul; it is the very essence of God in us. The paramount role of our spiritual self is its ability to connect with God. This connection affords us with an awareness that extends beyond the tangible world. Some of us identify this awareness as gut feelings or a knowing; this level of knowledge is acquired without the use of our intellect.

Usually, our intellectual self would deny this type of knowledge because it did not originate it and because this information is seldom logical. As a result, our spiritual self most often communicates this type of knowledge with our emotions first, where it takes on the identity of an unexplained feeling or urge. If this feeling is accepted within our emotional self, it may be successful at convincing our intellect to consider its instructions. The process of allowing ourselves to be led by the spirit may be instantaneous, take a lifetime or never occur.

For a moment, recall an occasion you had a gut feeling or a knowing about a situation. Was that feeling correct? How many times have you said, "I wish I had listened to my gut?" That's your divinity. It's the essence of God living inside you and leading you to all truth; your connection to everything that is divine and it is never wrong. You were born with this ability. The only occasions your gut feelings fail you is when you allow your emotional self to cloud the message, which is usually due to the existence of a *hidden pain*.

Have you ever felt terrible when you chose to ignore a gut feeling? Often these feelings are misinterpreted as guilt; however, most often it is your spiritual self attempting to teach you how to receive and follow its leadership. Perhaps the ultimate purpose of religious organizations is to enhance the volume of our spiritual self and teach us how to allow its influence to guide us towards finding more fulfillment in life.

In addition to seeking the assistance of religious organizations to enhance our willingness to be led by our spiritual self, we must take individual responsibility for our growth and knowledge of spiritual truths. Today we live in wireless always-on age that can easily drown out the voice of our spiritual self; therefore, we must be even more diligent in our efforts to escape from the noise. It is vital that we find ways to quiet our intellectual self on a regular basis. By no means does this imply we should minimize the significance of our intellect or abandon our ability to reason to seem more "spiritual." However, sometimes the volume of our intellectual self is too loud, and the process of quieting it is a necessary step towards improving the balance within *the triangle of the soul*.

Often the reasons we feel overwhelmed, stressed and drained in life is because we fail to exercise our right and divine ability to temporarily disconnect from most of the demands of this world. Regardless of the roles we play, we all need to temporarily disconnect from them, quiet our intellect and emotions, and tune into our spirit. Sometimes we use artificial stimulation to create the illusion of *quiet time*. The most notorious perpetrators are our televisions and other forms of entertainment. The effects of simultaneous audio-visual stimulation on our soul's balance are more powerful than we understand. These constant bombardments distort the balance within *the triangle of the soul*, and make it difficult to clearly hear the voice of our spiritual self. For some, the energy of our thoughts and emotions are distracted away from receiving solutions to real-life challenges and desires.

We all have an inherent need to temporarily disconnect ourselves from the external world. Unfortunately, we seldom do it correctly, which is why we often find ourselves constantly searching for fulfillment in life. The most common methods of quieting our world are praying or meditating. However, other activities that free you from thinking can be effective. Tasks that are generally repetitive in nature, relatively simple, and require a degree of solitude may provide you with the means to connect with your spiritual self on some level. Whenever you decrease external stimulation, the voice of your spirit will be amplified.

Have you ever experienced an occasion when the answer to a question or a revelation was suddenly revealed to you? Most likely, during that time you were engaged in a peaceful or simple activity that did not require your full attention. During that time the voices of your intellectual and emotional selves were quieter.

Make a commitment to schedule an activity that will allow you to escape from the daily bombardment of noises and obligations that inundate your life. It does not have to be a grand endeavor, nobody has to know, and it doesn't have to require a great deal of time. The goal is to simply allow yourself a few moments to tune into the voice of your spiritual self. The world will not end if you removed yourself from it for a short time! Trust me, I thought my world would, but it didn't, and neither will yours.

*A key to finding more fulfillment in life is to regularly engage in an activity that nurtures your spiritual self.* Is there a hobby, craft, or other activity that you enjoy doing? Perhaps one of the reasons it brings about enjoyment is because it allows your spiritual self to advance to a higher place within the triangle of your soul.

The next time you begin your favorite activity, be deliberate about insulating yourself from as much artificial stimulation as possible. Then, through your spiritual self's connection to the Creator simply ask God to speak to you. As you immerse yourself in your activity, listen for the voice of your spirit. It may not happen immediately, but over time as more balance is enhanced within the triangle of your soul and you will then begin to realize the presence of God.

Allowing yourself to be led by your spirit can sometimes be confusing or unsettling because it may seem to defy logic (intellectual self) and it may remove a certain level of comfort from your life (emotional self). Additionally, the process of submitting to the influences of your spiritual self may be difficult at first, simply because many of us have spent a lifetime ignoring its presence. During these challenges, faith is necessary.

You may recall the story of when Jesus spat onto a handful of dirt to make mud, which He rubbed onto the eyelids of a blind man.

Then He told the blind man to make his way to a pool on the other side of the town to wash it out. After the man washed the mud off his eyelids, he received sight. Jesus' act seemed to be completely illogical and it most likely diminished the man's level of comfort. Faith was required in order for the man to fully experience the Creator, so must it be for you.

Since our emotional self is the closest link to our spiritual self, it can easily be mistaken as the voice of our spirit. This occurrence is of great concern because one of the primary roles of our emotional self is to provide us with ongoing comfort. As a result, misinterpreted urges derived from our emotional self (the keeper of our hidden pains) can lead us to take actions that may seem divine or spiritual, but are actually self-servicing. An approach that may help you to discern whether you are hearing from your spiritual or emotional self is to consider the nature of the Creator.

We are made in the image of a Creator who intends leaving a soul experience maximum fulfillment in life. The Creator will not instruct us to take actions that will cause pain to anyone, especially for our own gains. Additionally, the Creator will not lead us to perpetuate ignorance or vexation of spiritual growth. In the image of the Creator, we lose our self-importance and connect with the whole of humanity. All actions led by the spirit will result in peace.

One of the most powerful drivers within our soul is passion. Like the red-hot coals that power a steam locomotive down its tracks, passion is an undeniable force that gives us the emotional strength to push through difficult challenges. It may be safe to say that passion is required to be successful in any endeavor. However, passion is an emotion. Passion is not divine nor is it spiritual. Like all other emotions, our passions can easily become self-serving; which is why they must be continually monitored and tested for their core intentions.

Under the disguise of being spiritual, our emotional self can lead us to judging others beyond the confines of established laws. We see this most often in the application of the self-righteous indignation. Remember, one of the primary goals of our emotional self is to maintain a certain level of comfort within the soul. As such, our emotions have the ability to compel us to persuade others into taking on views that make us feel more comfortable while minimizing its negative impact on others. Actions such as these are an indication of a deficiency of our spirit's influence within *the triangle of the soul*.

The fact that your spiritual self is the essence of the Creator living inside you makes you the most powerful being in the world. Continually acknowledge and cherish the spirit inside of you. Embrace the vital necessity of developing the awareness of your spiritual self – you will be amazed at the results.

# Power to Impact the World

# Power to Impact the World

Your power to impact the world exists in both an intangible and tangible form. Its intangible form is the energy you create while its tangible form is the gifts or talents you share with the world.

Let's begin with exploring how our intangible power impacts the world first. It is important we understand that the essence of God exists within the triangle of our souls in the form of our spiritual self.

This essence gives our souls the power to create. We read earlier a primary reason we identify God as the Creator is because only God can create something from nothing; within this definition, you have creative powers. In fact, you create the most powerful and rare substances in the Universe. From nothing, you create substances of love, hope, faith, hate, doubt, resentment the list is endless. For a moment allow this concept to find a place within you. Let us use the substance of love. Its power is undeniable. The love you present to this world is uniquely yours; others have loved, but no other being can love something or someone the way you can. More deeply at your birth, you were not innately equipped to love many of the people, or things your now apply that power towards, you created it.

Although we label most of these words as emotions a more accurate description may be to call them feelings. A feeling is not solely relegated to our emotional self; it is more of the union of all three parts of our soul working together. When David wrote in Psalms 139:14, "I am fearfully and wonderfully made," it was not a declaration of the brilliance of his physical features. Other creatures walk somewhat upright; have similar facial features, possess and demonstrate levels of intelligence and emotions. However, only humans possess a spiritual, emotional, and intellectual connection to our world. The triangle of your soul is the reason you are fearfully and wonderfully made; your power to impact the world.

Our ability to impact the world spans beyond our intentions. Even slight or seemly insignificant interaction has an impact; sometimes these impacts are even more profound because we share them unaware. Recall a situation when a stranger did something that was seemly disrespectful to you. Your response added impact and energy to that moment. Whether your response was positive or negative, you possessed and generated the power to impact.

Every thought, emotion, spiritual connection to God and others bring intangible power into the tangible reality. The power you create within *the triangle of your soul* forms a field of energy around you and emits power. Some may call it a blessing, others good luck, favor or reaping and sowing, the words you use are not more important than the concept. The concept is simply the greatest powers you create will always prevail in your life.

You are a unique expression of the Creator. *Throughout all of the times, past or to come there will never be another YOU!* You exist specifically to occupy now. There is no such thing as a "bad day" or a "good day". Every moment of your life belongs to you. The gift of life is a present that has been given to you to experience, enjoy and share your uniqueness to impact the world. Everything you do impacts the world; the breath you take, the space you occupy, every living and non-living creation is profoundly impacted by the presence of you. You matter! Whether you accept these facts or not, it is irrelevant; your mere existence impacts the world.

However, your truest power to impact the world does not derive from your physical existence. Your truest power resides within the triangle of your soul. This power was placed inside your soul the moment you received the breath of life. The breath of life is the essence of the Creator existing in the triangle of your soul; we know it as our spiritual self. In other words, you were born with a divine-supernatural *power to impact the world.* You have superpowers!

Within the *triangle of your soul,* you have the God-given ability to create the most powerful substances in the Universe. You create substances such as love, faith, hope as well as, anger, hatred, and resentment. Although we sometimes feel others present us with the opportunity to express these energies we are their ultimate creators. Remember, every moment of your life you are adding energy to the Universe, and you decide if it is positive or negative.

For some, our power to impact the world presents itself as a gift, talent or special affinity towards performing a task. However, your innate ability is much more divine than its external expression. Remember your power originated from the Almighty; as such your power to impact the world has divine significance. *A key to finding more fulfillment in life* is contributing your divine power to impact the world.

Some of us discount our divine power to impact the world because we focus too greatly on its material benefits. Our intellectual self can only measure the value of our power to impact the world solely on its ability to support our basic need for survival. Additionally, on its own, our emotional self can only measure the importance of our power to impact the world solely on its ability to provide us comfort. Spend a few moments of *quiet time* and ask yourself whether you've fully embraced your power to impact the world with your gifts or have you denied or augmented the truest nature of your divine power to make it be more socially acceptable or mostly bring you increased material gain.

Your power to impact the world may not make you popular nor support you financially, but it is vital and needed. In fact, the universe requires the contribution of your power to function properly. All of our societal chaos and pain are linked to our collective denial of using our divine powers to impact the world. Your divine ability is the conduit through which God uses to exercise power.

Take a few moments of *quiet time* and imagine you have unlimited resources and the ability to give (not receive) anything you desire to the world. List whatever you envision yourself giving the world. When you've finished, review your list. What common theme or themes do you see? Now summarize your vision, in other words give it a title. At some point during this exercise, it may have been realized that the essence of that vision has been with you for as long as you can remember; that's because it has been with you since your birth. Your spiritual self has been working to reveal this vision within your soul your entire life. Even more, the universe has been constantly bringing opportunities or lessons into your life in an attempt to help you bring your *power to impact the world* into full bloom.

Since this is such a powerful life-changing moment in your life, we must dig deeper into how you can bring your vision(s) or divine power to impact the world into a greater reality. Once again, resist the urge to discount your power because they may not seem to be able to support you financially or because of their perceived value in society. Instead, embrace your power for what it truly is; divinely yours. Your power to impact the world belongs to you, and no other being can impact the world the way you can. Embrace that fact! For a moment, spend quiet time and allow your spiritual self to speak to your thoughts and emotions. Allow your spirit to embrace your soul with purpose and meaning – power. During these moments try not to label your power to impact the world, just allow it to be. *A key to finding more fulfillment in life is embracing your power to impact the world.*

Now that you've come to embrace your power to impact the world your next step is to enhance your awareness. Enhancing your awareness of your power is easy; you simply need to think about it. For a moment think about your ears. Most likely you suddenly felt or sensed their presence the moment you thought of them. They didn't miraculously appear; they were always there, nothing changed except your thoughts. Now use the same process to increase the awareness of your power to impact the world. Like your ears your powers are always there and are supporting you on some level, and slightest focus will enhance their power the find more fulfillment in life.

Thoughts play an important role in helping us enhance the awareness of our powers, but it is vitally important we do not allow our intellectual self to dictate how we should use our powers to impact the world. Remember, one of the primary purposes of our intellectual self is to keep us connected to the external world; therefore, our intellectual self's overwhelming inclination is to use our powers to enhance our worldly status. Instead, understand the wisdom of the process, which is this, your ears exist and function without your focus of thought; however thoughts enhance your awareness of their existence and functionality. Thinking about your power to impact the world enhances your awareness of it and ability to bring it into reality.

Now let's bring your awareness into a functional reality. Start a new page in your notepad; on the top briefly describe or label one of your visions of powers to impact the world. Although you were created with an innate ability to uniquely impact the world, you must develop your ability to effectively utilize it.

One of the first action steps you must take is to increase your knowledge. Yes, you were born with that God-given power to impact the world, but you must learn how to use it effectively. This means spending *quiet time* studying, reflecting and developing your gift. You need to connect with people and teaching tools that will help you develop. Take a moment and write the name of at least one person and teaching tool you will reach out to concerning your gift. Then write the date you will reach out to them next to their names.

Now, develop a simple plan of action on how you will immediately contribute your impact to the world. If your power to impact the world does not currently support you financially or fit easily into your daily responsibilities, start small...very small! Some of us may have tried to contribute our impacts to the world in the past but became overwhelmed or frustrated because we took on more than the time and space allowed. This book, (one of my impacts on the world) began as one thought written on a piece of scrap paper over twenty-five years ago.

*Words spoken aloud are the key to finding more fulfillment in life.* Most religious and spiritual teachings recognize that the secret of creation is within words spoken aloud, "And God said let there be.". Use the authority of your words to focus your power to impact the world. Read your action plan a few times aloud. There is creative power in your words. Many of us already know that they impact the seen external world, the unseen spiritual word; however reading aloud engages our intellectual and emotional selves through audio-visual stimulation. Next, keep your action plan simple. It's perfectly fine if your plan of action is no more than a few sentences. Keep your plan near you and read it often. Stay flexible, because it will change as you develop your knowledge and skills. Also be open to embracing opportunities when they present themselves, remember you spoke words of creation regarding your plan. Once again, start small!

We read in the chapter titled *Emotional Self* that our emotions serve to obtain and maintain a certain level of comfort within the soul. Additionally, our emotions also have the awesome ability to transmit and receive the emotional energy of others. Have you ever walked into a room where people were dealing with an intense situation, and you could feel the tension? You might not have known the specifics of the problem, but you could feel something was wrong. Equally astounding is the fact that emotions can be received across living beings. When I was a little boy, our family dog would act somber in my presence when I was on punishments; somehow, he knew I was in trouble.

Your emotional self impacts the world around you. A key to finding more fulfillment in life is accepting the fact, you *have the absolute power to decide how you feel about every situation in your life, and your feelings have a direct impact on the outcome of that situation.*

At one point in my life, I had a job I did not like. I disliked Sunday evening because it meant I had to wake to Monday morning and go to that job. Some of my co-workers did not like me, nor I them. Despite being qualified and experienced for the job I got marginal performance reviews. During one of my worst days at work, my voice of reason (spiritual self) told me that I was "that guy". Perhaps you work with him or her; they are the person who is always complaining about their job. They are easily frustrated whenever it seems something is not working in their favor. That person is often overbearingly sarcastic and seems to be constantly trying to prove they are right and how much everyone else is wrong, especially management. They are usually alone at work or hang out with like-minded, miserable, complaining co-workers who regard themselves as being smarter and hardworking than everyone else.

I was shocked and embarrassed when I received that revelation and decided to make an immediate change. I did not draw it out with a pithy resolution to myself, nor did I tell anyone; I simply chose to change how I felt about my job. Over time, I began to find some parts of my job that I liked and consequently excelled at them, and when I encountered areas that needed improvements, solutions seemed to miraculously come to me. Slowly, I transformed from being "that guy" to becoming "the guy". Co-workers I only saw in passing introduced themselves to me; others sought me out for advice and saw me as a leader. Then it happened; my manager called me into his office and informed me the company was expanding another department and that I was chosen to be one of its managers. I didn't apply neither was I interviewed for the job, simply chosen. Wow! I went from the person nobody wanted to be around to a leader who had influence and respect. Success came into my life when I changed the energy I was generating from within my emotional self. In other words, I utilized my *power to impact the world*.

Let's uncover how my *power to impact on the world* worked within *the triangle of the soul* in that situation. First, I had to listen to the voice of my spiritual self. For some time my spirit had been giving me critical feedback about me negatively, and finally, I listened. Next, I forced my emotional self to receive those influences without placing blames, I took complete ownership of my feeling; as a result, I felt ashamed. Motivated by the revelation of shame and the desire to be successful, my intellectual self accepted the voice of my spirit and went into action to improve my situation.

### POWER TO IMPACT THE WORLD

Has your spiritual self been giving you critical feedback on how you may be negatively impacting the world? Right now, take some *quiet time* and ask your spiritual self to reveal any areas of your life that need to change. Any revelations you receive are not guilt but direction. Guilt is the reactive feeling we experience after willfully choosing to take incorrect actions. Direction is proactive guidance that leads us towards correct actions and more fulfillment in life.

Proverbs 23:7 states, "Such as a person thinks in their heart, so will they become." In this passage, the word heart refers to the soul, *the triangle of the soul*. This means you'll need all three parts of your soul to impact the world and your life.

God created you with the power to alter many of the negative situations in your life simply by taking responsibility for how you feel and think about them. Even more, your spiritual self has the awesome ability to summon the power of the Divine to help you in the areas of your thoughts and emotions that you cannot change alone. However, it all starts with. The word "attitude" comes to mind! Your attitude towards a situation has a tremendous impact on the results you receive.

> **Comment [T]:** This sentence seems incomplete.
> Revise for a better readability.

Let's get to work enhancing your positive impact on the world. If you have not done this yet take a few moments of *quiet time* and identify one situation in your life that you are unhappy with or that your spiritual self has been calling on you to change. In a few words write down what you think about that situation. In another section write all of your feelings regarding that situation. Now, review the words you wrote. These words represent the energy you contribute to that situation, whether positive or negative they are its primary source of power within your life.

Since you are the generator of the power of that situation in your life, you have control over it. Each negative word you wrote to describe your situation has an equally powerful opposite positive word. Review your list and write down the opposite of the first word that comes to you beside each negative word. Don't slow down to contemplate or search for the best word, just write. Once you have completed writing your new words, cross out the negative words to the extent they are no longer legible. Now all that remains are your new – positive words. These words are the foundation that will change your attitude towards that situation. Say these new words at least once a day. No need to reason why or make it an arduous task just say them aloud; the triangle of your soul needs to hear them. Over time your attitude and impact on the world regarding that situation will change – it has to!

"You are fearfully and wonderfully made." The word *fearful* denotes respect. The world respects or yields to whatever has the power to change it. According to the book of Genesis we were created to subdue the earth, in other words, we were created to impact the world. Lightning is respected because of the power it unleashes!

Lightning is in you! Embrace the fact that the Creator has made you to impact the world. The world is waiting to yield itself to you. You are *wonderful* because you were born with God-given gifts that only you can add to the world.

You were NOT created to hold on to empty hopes, wishful imaginations, or fickle luck to survive in this world. You were created to impact, enjoy, and appreciate every day the Creator gives you. What is that thing inside of you that seems to be compelling you to do more good for humanity and amplify the illumination of the glory of God? Name it - claim it! Do not allow another moment to transpire without you taking at least some small step towards unleashing your power to impact the world. Your impact may not bring you riches or fame, but it will bring you peace, joy, happiness, purpose – more fulfillment in life.

The world needs your IMPACT!

## POWER OF FAITH

A key to finding more fulfillment in life is understanding that *faith is your divine ability to create reality.* Faith is a combination of hopes (emotional self) and beliefs (intellectual self) working together within *the triangle the soul.* Your spiritual self does not give you faith; it serves to guide and enhance your faith. Faith is an emotional and intellectual decision. Since your birth, your spiritual self has been aware of the Creator, and it has never stopped working to help you experience God more deeply. However, first, you had to intellectually learn and emotionally accept its teachings before beliefs became a possibility. Even now, you choose to accept portions of your beliefs or religion that cannot be explained – that acceptance begins with believing, which leads to faith.

For a few moments, let's dig deeper into how faith works within *the triangle of the soul.* Hope is an emotion, and therefore resides within your emotional self. We know that our emotional self is indiscriminate as to what stimulates it and will accept any situation as long as it provides some sort of comfort. Once our emotional self becomes fixed upon receiving more of a situation, it works to convince our intellectual self to desire it as a tangible substance. Once our intellectual self has been convinced to desire or expect a situation to become a substance, it engages in the powerful process of believing. This process is neutral. Meaning it works to bring both positive and negative situations into our lives; all things are possible if-when you believe!

Remember our overweight friend in the chapter titled, *Dealing with Depression*? They described themselves as feeling like a failure when it came to their ability to deal with their weight challenges. Within their emotional self, failure had become a feeling they accepted as being a part of their character, and sadly, that feeling convinced their intellectual self into believing the same message. As a result, achieving their goal is nearly impossible. They believed themselves to be a failure at changing their body; in fact, they had faith in it!

Of course this person did not intend to use the power of faith to lock themselves into struggling with their weight; nevertheless, they used its power to bring that reality into their life. How often do we unwittingly use our power of faith to bring realities into our lives we do not desire?

Consider the words written in Hebrews 11:1 KJV, "*Now* faith *is* the *substance* of things *hoped* for, the evidence of things *not seen*." In other words, faith is an actual substance created by our hopes; it is so powerful that it can bring situations into existence that did not or perhaps were not intended to exist. Additionally, faith starts the process of bringing things into reality immediately (now faith), even though we may not immediately realize them.

We now know that the *power of faith* is neutral and we use its power in every aspect of our lives. We build relationships with the faith they will result in our benefit. We educate ourselves; work, and play all with the faith they will enhance our lives. The unconscious use of faith comes and flows easily throughout our daily lives. However, the power of our faith is challenged when we attempt to apply it to situations that contend against whatever seems impossible. We call these challenges doubt.

Doubt is more than merely the opposite of faith; it damages the soul's ability to have faith. Doubt drains our vitality and joy and locks us into a world of fear and regret. It chains us away from wholly experiencing the power of the Creator in our lives. Since doubt is such a fearsome challenger, it would be prudent to spend time examining how it works, where it comes from and how to release ourselves from its grip.

Let's begin by examining an occasion when it seemed your faith failed you. Think about a situation you really wanted to result in your favor, but did not. You had your hopes up high. You did everything right; perhaps you prayed, believed, planned and visualized your victory. However, it seemed your faith was not powerful enough to produce the results you had placed so much of your soul's energy into. How did that tragic disappointment make you feel? It probably hurt more than you could describe.

As a result of that disappointment, a few things immediately went into action within the triangle of your soul. Your intellectual self began to develop reasons why your faith seemed to fail. It may have surmised that your intended outcome wasn't in your best interest, it may have identified blame, or perhaps it provided your soul with constructive feedback and ideas on how to be more effective in the future. Whichever approach your intellectual self took (perhaps a combination of both); your intellectual self turned that disappointment into a memory. Remember, one of your intellect's jobs is to keep you connected and functioning in this world. Remaining functional would be difficult if your thoughts were stuck replaying that disappointment. Your intellectual self is able to process most of life's disappointments through its power of reasoning, regardless of whether the basis of its reasoning is based on facts that are true or false. The result is that your intellectual self learned from that disappointing experience.

Unlike your intellectual self, your emotional self experienced the intensity of that painful disappointment more deeply. Depending on the intensity of the pain, your emotional self might not have been able to fully process that event as a life lesson, especially if the outcome did not seem fair. As a result, your emotional self stored away the pain it could not process.

Over time, unprocessed painful events will begin to gain energy and find a place within our souls. If this process is not recognized and dealt with, it becomes a *hidden pain*. We know that hidden pains can last a lifetime. If we do not uncover and heal ourselves from the pain of disappointment, it will negatively affect the effectiveness of our faith for the rest of our lives. These *hidden pains* protect themselves by enacting the powerful emotion of fear; in this case, the fear of experiencing the disappointment of another unanswered prayer. The fear of using faith is doubt. The longer we live with *hidden pains* caused by an unanswered prayer, the more powerful fear (doubt) becomes. A major reason why we are more faithful and hopeful when we are children is that pain has not convinced us to doubt.

As a means of protecting us from the possibility of re-experiencing the pain of disappointment, our emotional self will take steps to soften the possibility of future pain. It accomplishes this by convincing our souls to embrace the possibility of failure; another unanswered prayer. For many of us, the willingness to outright embrace failure (doubt) is too difficult to accept; therefore, our emotional self convinces our intellect to camouflage these feelings through its process of reasoning.

Reasoning is our intellectual self's ability to take logical steps to ensure our functionality in this world. Reasoning or being reasonable is vital to our survival in the tangible world; however, logic or reasoning is powerfully opposed to the intangible. Reasoning is not an enemy of the intangible. Our intellectual self relies on facts or the illusions to function, as such, on its own it can only loosely relate to the nonfactual, intangible God. Alone our intellect cannot develop the amount of faith necessary to release its power.

Doubt, empowered by fear, is our emotional self's attempt at trying to protect us from the possibility of being disappointed in the event our faith does not produce the outcome we desire. In other words, *we doubt to protect ourselves from the possibility of being disappointed.*

Yes, it's obvious that we enhance the power of our faith when we remove doubt, but what is less obvious is how to remove or at least reduce our doubts. A key resides in uncovering *hidden pains*. While you were reading this chapter, a past event may have recalled itself to you. If nothing has come to you, take a moment and recall a situation whereby you intensely hoped, perhaps prayed, and had faith in a desired outcome; but received the opposite. Does the memory of that disappointment still hurt you in some way? Most likely it does, which is why it surfaced so quickly. Allow those feelings to surface; they are *hidden pains*! Now, bookmark this page, go back to the *Healing from Hidden Pains* chapter of this book, and go to work!

# POWER OF FAITH....MORE

Faith is a substance, an actual element that we control. Faith has the ability to bring situations that currently do not exist into reality; faith is a creative power. In this book, God is often referred to as the Creator because only God can create something out of nothing. The essence of the Creator exists within each of us through our spiritual self. Therefore, the ultimate power of our faith relies on our spirit's link with the Creator.

Remember your spiritual self's link to God is not one-way, you talking to God only, it is also the means through which God talks to you. Through this connection, we can be led towards ideas and activities that support the Divine. Perhaps a major reason many of our prayers are not answered is we neglect to follow the leading of our spiritual self, our connection to God. In other words, would we have even made many of our requests to God if we were truly following the leading of our spiritual self?

Prayer spoken aloud activates the divine nature of faith and gives it direction. Submitting prayer requests is our ability to influence the power of God. Yes, prayer supported by spiritually led faith is that powerful! The purpose of making prayer requests is to ask God to do something we are not able to do on our own.

Consider this; most of us plan to pay our monthly expenses using a predictable income. For the most part, our funds are allocated towards a predetermined purpose. Now imagine you support a child who unexpectedly informs you just before bedtime they need money for an important school project and the money is due tomorrow morning. In response, you reallocate a portion of the money you plan using for something else to fulfill the child's unplanned need. In other words, their request alters your plans. You aren't purposefully withholding funds from the child, nor punishing them; you don't give them the money solely because they don't ask for it.

In the previous chapter, we learned to remove the doubts we must uncover and heal from the hidden pains of unanswered prayers. It does not stop there. Faith is also empowered by our thoughts. To have our prayers realized, we must diligently rebuke any thoughts that can hinder their success. Therefore, we must be constantly aware of our thoughts.

Embrace the truth that you are a reflection of your thoughts. Your thoughts are the greatest conduit of power within *the triangle of the soul*. Your thoughts are so powerful that your world transforms itself to conform to them. Many of us fail to realize how much seemingly innocent thoughts negatively affect our faith. In the next ten seconds, think of five people you feel are much more favored in life than you. Do you see them? Was it difficult to imagine five people? If so, great! If their names came quickly and easily to you, it might be of some concern. Here's why. Such thinking is an indication that your intellectual self believes others are more blessed, lucky, favored or perhaps even better than you. It is impossible to fully utilize the power of your faith when you think you are less deserving. You must believe you are worthy.

No other person in all of creation is more important to you and your relationship with the Creator – nobody! Yes, other people may display advanced skills compared to yours, or may be enjoying greater successes in life, but they are not innately better than YOU! They are not more loved by God than you. The Universe does not favor one life over another; every life is important and has significance – YOUR LIFE!

According to the teachings of Jesus, we do not need a lot of faith to activate the *power of faith*; faith the size of a mustard seed is enough. A seed represents the potential of what could be; it has to grow before it can bear fruit. Is it possible the reason some of us do not receive the results of our prayers is we have not grown our faith to that level?

*A key to finding more fulfillment in life is understanding that faith has to grow!* Growth takes time. Some areas of faith grow quicker than others. The rate growth in areas of our faith is unique for each of us because our life experiences, knowledge, and understanding influence our individual abilities to believe in the Divine.

Properly planted seeds grow best during the showers of rain and the heat of the sun. As such, your seed of faith will experience its best growth when battling these elements. The battle is in your thoughts and emotions and their ability to believe against disbelief;

hope beyond hopelessness. *Faith grows strong through constant use and out of struggle.*

A seed cannot bear fruit before it is ready. If it is going to require faith to make your dreams a reality, you will need to grow your faith to those levels first.

Imagine a person who has decided to join a fitness gym for the first time. Upon joining the gym, they decide one of their goals is to be able to lift one hundred pounds. Currently, they are nowhere near being able to lift that much weight. However, they are diligent at exercising with the weights they can currently handle. Over time their ability to lift more weight increases. Until one day, it happens; they are exercising with one hundred pounds of weight.

Here is the "mustard seed" truth to that story. That person already had the muscles they needed to lift one hundred pounds; they just were not strong enough. Again, the potential (seed) was always there. Sure, the path to growing stronger was painful, perhaps lonely at times and they encountered many challenges and setbacks, but each time they exercised their muscles they became a little stronger. The power of faith increases when you use it, and like the person at the gym, at first, you may need to start small.

Equally important, you must put a concentrated effort into learning how to effectively exercise your faith. There are a small group of people (I don't know them personally) who like to visit the gym around the same time as I. Over time, I began to wonder why it seemed some of the people at the gym improved their physical fitness and overall look while others seemed to remain the same. We all shared similar levels of commitment and used the same equipment. Curious, I observed the people who did not seem to be progressing and realized a common theme, they seldom excercised properly. Either they hadn't been taught proper exercising technique, or they chose to ignore the teachings. In other words, they did not receive nor hear the words that would have increased their effectiveness in the gym. Faith comes by hearing!

A key to finding more fulfillment in life, *is committing yourself to hearing words that will increase your faith.* Words of faith have the power to enhance your connection to God. Words of faith inspire and motivate us to go against the fear of failure or pain of possible disappointment. They smother words and feelings of doubts within the soul and equip us with divine knowledge and abilities. Words of faith teach and help us understand that all things are possible when we dare to believe.

The final observation I noticed about the people at the gym who didn't seem to be progressing was that usually they hung out together at the gym. They rarely reached out to or even extended a greeting to the people who were having more success. Yes, reaching out and getting exercise advice from the people at the gym who were more successful seemed like an obvious thing to do, but it also seemed to be the most difficult. We won't labor over the reasons why these groups kept to themselves; we will only take its lesson. *To grow the power of your faith, you must surround yourself with people who are faithful; even if you are seemingly the "weakest" person in the group.*

Now you are at a critical moment in this chapter. Ask yourself this question, "Do I associate with the people, places, and activities that enhance the power of my faith or hinder it? Take a moment of *quiet time* with this question. Your spiritual self is speaking to you; listen!

Throughout our life's experiences, we will have disappointments, find ourselves placed in unfair situations and have our faith weakened. At times using the power of our faith to find more fulfillment life will sometimes seem hopeless. Nevertheless, a horrific tragedy is to decide to live a frustrated and unfulfilled life because we are afraid to regularly use the awesome *power of faith.*

An unanswered prayer does not mean we are unloved by the Creator nor does it indicate failure. It may be an indication that something is out of balance within *the triangle of the soul* and perhaps your life; perhaps you are asking for the wrong things. Or maybe you have not grown your faith to the level of receiving the results of that prayer. Even more, the things you've applied the power of your faith towards are on the way – you just have to be patient. Spend some *quiet time* with the Creator to uncover your reasons.

Whatever the reason, through the leading of your spiritual self you have the divine ability to utilize the power of your faith and find more fulfillment in life.

# GUARD YOUR SOUL

Throughout our journey in this book, we have uncovered keys on how to heal, enhance, and inspire our souls; now it is time to protect it. Some of us were taught or prefer to believe that we have at least one angel who was appointed by God to watch over us. On some levels that may be true; however, you are primary the guardian of *the triangle of your soul*. The reasons are simple; for the most part, you decide what your intellect learns and thinks about as well as which emotions you allow to dominate your feelings. Even more, you have complete control over the level of influence you allow your spiritual self to have within your soul and its level of connection with the Creator.

Is it possible we have not guarded our souls as well as we should? Perhaps the reasons we sometimes hear negative voices much louder and clearer is because we innocently allow them to pass our guard. A devil cannot be completely credited for pulling us away from the Creator; many times we do it to ourselves. But how?

When we listen to music, watch television programs or engage in other forms of entertainment and recreation they stimulate either or both of our emotional and intellectual selves. On the surface, many of these activities are innocent, healthy, and needed. To fully enjoy these activities we must allow them to freely enter *the triangle of the soul*; in other words, they are given a place within our souls. Herein is the possible danger! During this course of submission, we willingly invite negative thoughts and evil into our souls.

We read earlier that your intellectual self never forgets and processes every experience you encounter. Also, your emotional self works to find some level of comfort within every situation. In other words, your thoughts and emotions are impacted by every experience they encounter; positive and negative.

Here is an example of how entertainment affects the soul. Imagine one of your favorite television programs features a character that you "love to hate". While observing that character's performance, your intellectual self is learning their character traits, regardless of whether you consciously approve of their actions, you are learning from them. Also, your emotions are being stimulated as they try to find comfort in your excitement about a character you know is acting in a manner that is wrong. Beyond your will or level of awareness, your emotional self will begin the process of convincing your soul to accept those actions. Unwittingly you have instigated a battle of negativity against the divine nature of your soul. The longer you expose yourself to that negative source, the more it gains strength, overpowers your divinity and makes you begin to conform to it. In other words, we accept it into our souls.

If this concept seems extreme, consider the following. The language, tone, accent, speed and the way you form sentences were developed to conform to the people who influenced you during your formative years. Even the level of expression of your laugh was formed by the information you received growing up. Have you ever visited another part of this Country or the world and initially found it difficult if not impossible to understand and speak their language? However, the longer you interacted and exposed yourself to that environment your ability to understand them increased. The longer you interacted with that group, they might have noticed, the more you began to mimic some of their cultural traits, mannerisms; you began to gain a better appreciation of their foods, and you might have even begun to somewhat dress like they. Most of these changes will occur without much effort on your part; it is your emotional and intellectual selves accepting what they are exposed to and applying it to your soul.

As you read this chapter it is likely your spiritual self will speak to you regarding situations you need to bring into moderation or completely refrain from. During those moments take some *quiet time* and write down whatever comes to you. Resist the urge to justify your participation in those activities. It does not matter if the items on your list are legal, socially acceptable or enjoyed by others. The only fact that matters is that it is hindering your ability to find more fulfillment in life.

Thousands of years ago the writer of Romans 7:21 shared a heartfelt struggle when he wrote: "Whenever I try to do good, it seems that evil is always present." Evil is not an actual being. It is anything that causes division between you and the Creator. It is a force that exists as the complete opposite of your divinity. And it maintains its existence through the suffering of your soul and the suffering you inflict on others - guard your soul!

Your spiritual self will never instruct you to harm yourself or other people nor cause suffering, especially among those who love and depend on you.  However, your spiritual self will warn and instruct you to minimize or eliminate your interaction with people, places, and activities that will harm your soul. *How you spend your free time and the company you keep are vital aspects to guarding your soul.* We have no choice but to be influenced by the people we interact with regularly, especially from those whom we choose to entertain ourselves with. The saying "You are the company you keep" is a powerful truth.

All three sides of the *triangle of the soul* are capable and vital contributors in guarding the soul. Our intellect provides us with the ability to understand and anticipate the potential impact of situations. While our emotions empower us with the ability to discern the intentions of others or a situation as it relates to our personal comfort. Most often we use our thoughts and emotions to determine whether a situation is for our greater good.

We now understand that both our thoughts and feelings are frequently self-centered and can be easily fooled; they need a balance. Our spiritual self is never affected by our thoughts and emotions and is the perfect balancer and lead guard within the soul. When we are in balance within the soul, the voice of our spiritual self comes in clear, and following its lead is effortless; some identify it as walking in the spirit. However, even when we choose to neglect the relationship of our spiritual self within the soul, it often finds a way to speak even louder when we are in danger or choose to participate in actions that will harm the soul. Some know its voice as the guilty feeling we experience when we are planning or perpetrating wrong actions. During those moments of unrest within your soul, take a moment and ask yourself, "What is my spirit trying to tell me? "As it is said, today, if you hear his voice, do not harden your hearts as in the rebellion." *Hebrews 3:15 English Standard Version.*

Regardless of the number of mistakes you might have made in the past be encouraged and empowered by the fact that you have the divine ability to effectively guard your soul. Your power over the external influences of evil is so awesome that simply by resisting evil, it will lose its ability to influence your soul. The key is resistance. The act of resisting evil's influences is solely your responsibility and actions you must continually take. However, the appearances of evil are not always apparent. Remember, evil is anything that causes division between you and the Creator. Sometimes that separation hides in activities or situations that are meant for our good. Be careful other relationships, possessions, positions of honor or responsibility do not take precedence over your connection with God. A simple yet hard truth is that everything in your life is temporary, you may choose to release things that no longer have value, or they choose to leave you, but your soul is eternally yours. God remains!

Rebuke evil when needed, but be careful your actions are not giving a place for evil to enter your soul; guard it! Whether it exists within our souls or the external world, every action we take must first find its place within our thoughts before it is manifested. Remember our intellectual self is our primary connection to this world; thoughts channel our divinity into this reality. Conversely, our reality is greatly defined by our thoughts, in other words, we become what we think about. It is impossible to have peaceful giving thoughts and be simultaneously mean and selfish. The state of our emotions is controlled by our thoughts. The next time you feel bad, a brief moment of *quiet time* and observe your thoughts.

The primary guard of the *triangle of the soul* is our intellectual self. Guard your thoughts, and your soul will be safe!

A reality of life is; there are some negative situations that must be experienced. During those times, rely on your spiritual self and its connection to the Creator to provide your thoughts and emotions with guidance and strength. Use the concepts you've learned throughout your journey in this book; establishing *quiet time*, *uncovering and dealing with hidden pains*, allow yourself to be led *by the spirit*, work on enhancing your ability to *impact the world*, believe in the *power of faith*. A guarded soul is sure to find more fulfillment in life.

# RECEIVING YOUR SOUL'S DESIRES

When we were children one of the most wonderful questions anyone could ask was, "What do you want to be when you grow up?" The very nature of that question implied we could grow to be anything we desired. When I was a boy, I wanted to be a pro-football playing-secret agent who won gold medals running track in the Olympics. Who did you want to be?

Moments after our birth one of the first needs is to have events work in our favor; this is called desire. Regardless of how simple or outlandish our visions of adulthood were as children, at the core of our imaginations were desires.

Primarily desires are developed through a combination of our emotional and intellectual selves working within *the triangle of the soul.* Our intellect measures the value of the things we want, and our emotions decide whether they will bring us comfort. Next, our emotional self gives us the impetus to pursue our desires while our intellect formulates a plan toward making (or keeping) them a reality. At the heart of some of our deepest disappointments and frustrations in life is facing the reality that a desire may not be fulfilled. Sometimes these hurtful feelings compound themselves when it seems other people are getting what they desire in life, especially when we have determined they are undeserving.

First, let's agree that no one gets their way all the time. As a person who believes in the unlimited power of the Creator; for many years I wondered why people who believe in God's teachings do not seem to have their desires met with any more frequency than non-believers.

The answer to this conundrum was simpler than I realized. The writer of the 37th chapter of Psalms indicated that as a result of delighting ourselves in the Lord, God would give us what we desire. Since this passage seems to reveal a vital key for finding more fulfillment in life, let's spend some time understanding this statement. To explore the numerous religious views on the correct way to solicit God's help is beyond the scope of this book. For now, let's simply assume the spiritual teaching found in Psalms 37:4 is available to anyone who believes and practices its principle.

The idea of having a delightful relationship with the Creator seems to contradict the general perception some may have concerning God. Growing up, I was taught to fear God and that on my own I was not worthy of God's love or help, and if I happened to receive God's favor with just one slip-up that favor was in jeopardy. It seemed God wasn't truly for me. I believed the Creator loved me in some inalienable way, but I wasn't sure God necessarily liked me. Those impressions stayed with me throughout most of my life. I wanted to have a better relationship with the Creator; however, those negative ideas had a firm place within my soul. As a result, the idea of having a delightful relationship with God seemed impossible. In fact, it was impossible. I was at an impasse. Either I could embrace the idea that my relationship with God could be a delight and that more fulfillment in this life was truly possible; or I could continue to believe I was a creature who would never be fully accepted by my Creator. I had to choose how I understood and received God; I had to challenge, rethink and even change some of my views of God.

The first step began with my understanding of love. I believed there was love that existed far beyond my understanding. A love that transcended all of space and time. A love so immensely perfect and bright no darkness created on my part could distinguish nor drive it way. It's a love that accepts me completely, where I am and the way I am – right now! I grabbed on to that idea and at times fought fiercely against moments when situations challenged me to think and feel differently. It's a love so complete that pure words cannot describe, but can only be felt within the soul – the love of God.

Take a few moments of *quiet time* and meditate on God's love for you. Allow whatever good feeling or thoughts that come to you enter your soul. But don't hold onto any particular feeling and thought, just let them flow at will. Sense their essence. If guilt or negative feelings enter also allow them to flow and allow the all-encompassing essence of God's love cleanse your soul.

Now that you've elevated your acceptance of God's awesome love for you it is time to accept a simple truth; your actions have a tremendous impact on the level you delight concerning your relationship with God.

Recall or imagine a relationship you would consider a delight (one that is pleasurable and enjoyable). That relationship is built on respect, honesty, understanding, acceptance and sharing quality time with each other. That relationship also has rules that incorporate themselves into the frame of your lives altogether. They revolve around perhaps remaining physically loyal, and require a certain level of emotional and intellectual loyalty towards each other. Whatever the rules, as long as they are reasonably met that relationship is good – a delight.

Is it possible the reason our relationship with the Creator is not as delightful as it should be is because we are not truly honoring our side of the relationship? Could it be that our struggle with God or the disruption we sometimes feel from our spiritual self is not condemnation but an indication that we are taking actions that are driving us away from a delightful relationship with God?

If you feel as though actions you have taken are hindering your relationship with God, don't dismay. Just as with any other relationship that's struggling or gone astray, a relationship with God can be repaired. The process of repairing your relationship with God is not much different than it is with any other broken relationship. In fact, it is much easier with God because God is your all-loving Creator. God wants to be the most important part of your life and is ready to receive you as you are. To humbly understand that truth will have an incredible impact on your soul.

Before that relationship can really take hold, you will need to uncover the *hidden pains* you caused or experienced from those past actions. We know from the chapter, *Uncovering Hidden Pains*. Wherever you are in life, you can go to God, humbly and openly identify your faults, ask for forgiveness, and replace your destructive actions with constructive ones.

A key to any delightful relationship is spending quality time with each other. God is a spirit; therefore, within *the triangle of the soul*, our closest connection to God is through our spiritual self. As you recall, the greatest opponent to our spiritual self (connection to the intangible) is our intellectual self (connection to the tangible); therefore, quality time with God requires pulling ourselves away from the external world.

When we are in a delightful relationship, we focus our energy on pleasing the other person. The best way to achieve that objective is to learn as much as possible about them. Also, we take great care to protect that relationship by avoiding any activities or habits that can jeopardize our union. Most of the rules, laws, or commandments concerning the Creator were not designed to oppress you but were developed to help you understand what God requires in a relationship.

For a moment, put this book down and ask your spiritual self to reveal at least one thing you are doing that is keeping your relationship with God from being more of a delight. List whatever items that come to you. The first thing that comes to you is the first thing you need to address. Yes, you may have several items on your list, but you have to start somewhere, right? Also, resist the urge to doubt the validity of the voice you just heard; reject the need to justify the reasons why it may be acceptable to continue those actions. Just give in, confess your faults, ask for forgiveness, and then ask for God's help. Next, commit yourself to changing your ways. You may not be able to quickly change every aspect of that situation, but it is vital that you take meaningful, consistent steps toward changing.

Notice the writer of Psalms 37 wrote delight "yourself" in the Lord. He did not write that the Lord had to find delight in you.

Perhaps that is because God already delights in you. Under normal circumstances, a newborn does not have to take correct actions before its parents love it, their love is instant and steadfast, and so it is with God.

Our greatest gift in life is that each day we have an opportunity to enhance our relationship with God. Your relationship with the Creator is personal. Just as no outside person has the right to dictate the personal rules of a friendship or intimacy between two people, no other person has the right or authority to dictate the rules to your personal relationship with God. However to ignore proven methods for communing with God would be foolish. Therefore, it is your responsibility to study and understand God's nature and commandments; it is your sole responsibility to ensure your relationship with God is a delight.

The psalmist also implied that because of having a delightful relationship with the Creator, God would, in turn, give us the things we desire. So why does it seem to occur so infrequently? Once again imagine a relationship you cherish. Initially, the two of you were somewhat awkward together, but as you spent more time together the level of understanding between the two of you grew. Until eventually, without saying a word, you could discern what the other was thinking. The two of you also got to a place where very often you regarded the other person's needs over your own. Additionally, you began to want the things that person wanted and liked more of what they liked; you even began to see the world through their eyes. You changed.

Here is the key to receiving the desires of your heart: as your relationship with the Creator develops, your desires will change, you *will begin to desire the things God also desires for you.* Some of the things that seemed critically important to you will lose their insignificance, while other things that were previously insignificant will mean the world to you.

Many of the desires that are currently in your heart are valid although some of them may be presenting themselves incorrectly. What do you desire in life? Take a few moments write down everything that comes to you. Be critically honest, do not try to justify or calculate the validity of your desires - just write.

The desires on your list fit into one of two categories. They are either the desires you want to receive or give. Review your list and indicate desires you want to receive with the letter "R" and desires you want to give with a letter "G". The desires you want to receive most likely originate from your intellectual self. Those you want to give most likely have a spiritual aspect to them. However, depending on your semantics some of the items on your list may be deceiving. For example, if you wrote, "I want the world to give me money," it may read like a giving desire but is, in fact, a receiving desire.

Every desire on your list is important to you; however, you must uncover whether pursuing or obtaining them will result in more fulfillment in your life. This chapter was placed near the end of this book in the hopes that once you arrived here you would have developed a much greater balance and understanding of the triangle of your soul. Once again, review your list, this time, spend some *quiet time* on each item, and focus on how the pursuit of each desire truly makes you feel within your soul. Draw a line through any desires that give you a negative feeling.

When a soul is more balanced deep internal feelings are not isolated to only our emotions, they encompass the complete *triangle of the soul.* Any negative feelings you experienced while reviewing your list is an indication that you should not pursue them; at least not at this time. Caution; if you are preparing to peruse desires that will intentionally harm the lives of the people God placed in your life you need to spend more *quiet time* with the Creator.

Ask your spiritual self for guidance on how to be in a place in life to receive your desires from the Creator. Yes, receiving the desires of your heart was promised to you but it is up to you to be ready to receive them; there will be work you will have to do first. There may be destructive activities that must be discontinued, or a new level of knowledge, understanding or skill you need to acquire; perhaps there are worldly relationships you need to develop or end.

Receiving the desires of your heart is the essence of finding more fulfillment in life. God seldom gives us definable timelines of when we will receive our desires, therefore trusting God and developing a delightful relationship whereby our awareness of the

Creator is developed and clear is paramount. The great news is you can receive your heart's desire; in fact, they exist just for you. However, before you can realize the desires of your heart and find more fulfillment in life you must first make your relationship with the Creator a delight.

# WHEN WE DIE

The greatest mystery of life is what happens when it ends, or at least seemingly ends within this reality. In this chapter we will refrain from highlighting any specific religious beliefs concerning how to enter paradise or avoid damnation. Instead, we will contemplate what happens to the existence of the soul *when we die*.

For a moment, imagine you are standing on the shore of a vast ocean. The ocean's currents are moving in harmony. Each rippling wave is starting where the other ends and flowing effortlessly to and from the shore. Now reach down, cup your hands together, and scoop out a handful of water from the ocean. Your action changes the volume and flow of the ocean; even more, the water you hold in your hands is now isolated.

A few moments ago the water you now hold in your hands was complete. It was known by all, it knew all, and was connected to all. The water you hold had neither true beginning nor end, it simply existed. But now it has become a self-contained unit; it has been separated from itself. Although the water in your hand still possesses the priorities of the ocean, its ability to flow has been greatly diminished. The water you hold in your hands misses its connection and has an inherent desire to return to completeness. It may spend a lifetime performing the duties of water, but it will never experience true fulfillment until it returns to its source.

Perhaps our souls are like that handful of water; removed from our source and placed inside human containers. Possibly our greatest need is to return to perfect unity with the Creator and each other in the vast ocean of paradise. Within the triangle of the soul, heaven is rejoining with all that is Divine. Conversely, hell is a soul that will never again experience infinite joy, peace, a fulfilled sense of connection to all. Hell is being eternally separated!

Loneliness is an uncontrollable desire to connect with others, but being unable. It is a burning pain that simultaneously afflicts all sides of the *triangle of the soul*; even your spiritual self can experience loneliness. Loneliness is one of the harshest states of existence to experience in life. Now, imagine being lonely forever; that is hell.

It is generally agreed that whatever the state of being we experience *when we die* we will be able to understand our condition. In order to interpret our condition, we will need our intellectual self active on some level. Furthermore, any feelings of joy or sorrow need to be interpreted through our emotions. Therefore, it is reasonable to surmise that both our current intellectual and emotional selves will continue to exist after death. Our spiritual self is fundamentally eternal; therefore, it will remain a part of who we shall be when we die.

The triangle of your soul is eternally you. The essence of who you are (your soul) will never end. However, you will transition into your true self. Your spiritual self will take its rightful place as the leader within your soul. Your emotional self will no longer carry the burden of constantly trying to maintain some sort of comfort at all costs; which means you will be free from your hidden pains. The need to compete and connect with temporary material things will no longer exist; therefore, our intellect will be free to realize its true genius.

It is reasonable to assume that we will know other ones *when we die*, however, our current relationship statuses will no longer be important. Neither will gender, age, language, skin color nor any of the trivial categories we hold on to in this world.

Live in awareness about the decisions and actions you take in this world. The Creator wants the triangle of your soul to return to its completeness and connection to all. From the moment of your birth to your death, God, the Creator, the Divine Almighty desires to connect with you...all of you.

*Living a life that continually enhances your connection to God is the ultimate key to finding fulfillment in life!*

Peace.

www.ingramcontent.com/pod-product-compliance
Lightning Source LLC
LaVergne TN
LVHW021601070426
835507LV00015B/1894